Even Broken-Winged Divas Can Fly

Living in an able-bodied world:
The continuing story of
Little Diva On Wheels

shalakopress.com

Even Broken-Winged Divas Can Fly

All rights reserved
© Copyright 2020 Jennifer Kuhns

The author has made every effort to contact and
acquire permission from all persons referenced or
mentioned in the autobiography.

Reproduction in any manner, in whole or part,
In English or any other language, or otherwise
without the written permission of publisher is prohibited.

For information contact Shalako Press
P.O. Box 371, Oakdale, CA 95361-0371

ISBN: 978-1-7340795-4-8

Cover Inspiration Jennifer Kuhns
Cover Art and Design Edward Luena
Formatting by Major Mitchell & Karen Borrelli
Editor Rofiah Breen

PRINTED IN THE UNITED STATES OF AMERICA

"This book, *Even Broken-Winged Divas Can Fly,* is inspirational and allows people to see the upside to all life's troubles. The author, Jennifer Kuhns, shares how wanting to live life and have life experiences, being part of something, compelled her to find a way to make it so. She shows how she was even able to do things healthy-bodied people cannot do."

Debbi Mitchell, RN

Dedication

To Debbie Franco and Becky Lyter who together spent eight years as my aides, school moms, partners in crime, (one who bought me my first drink and one who took me on my first amusement park ride), and who still remain two of my dearest friends.

I'd like to add a thank you to Craig who wasn't always crazy about having his mom at school…all the time.

EVEN BROKEN-WINGED DIVAS CAN FLY

It is exhausting being a diva. I mean the clothes, the hair, the makeup, the pierced ears . . .times four, BTW (gotta stay ahead of my peers), and spending all the time that goes along with it, trying to be like everyone else while being a diva about it, not to mention, a trend setter.

Entering high school in the fall of 1994, I soon realized, brought changes, changes in focus, changes in what was important, changes in attitude, and changes in how I opted to do things. I'm not saying I threw make-up and stylish clothing out of the window, but for some reason I kind of found a niche of my own. I didn't feel the need to replicate what everyone else was wearing. Okay, I had Rockies like most everyone else . . .purple Rockies were my fav, but I wasn't driven by my need or desire to belong or be accepted through my outward appearance. Purple just happened to be my favorite color.

Staying ahead of the game was still part of my modus operandi, though. As a disabled person I learned from an early age that I had to do and be better than everyone else just to be on an equal playing field. Sounds weird, I know, but sadly it's true. The funny part about that, once you have proven yourself and are considered an equal, you are then often called an overachiever. Damned if you do and damned if you don't.

Soap box rant over . . .maybe. I began to look at and see things differently because high school was, to begin with, overwhelming and all encompassing. There was less "home time." What time was spent at home was less about therapies, home, and family stuff, and more about preparing and doing stuff for school like homework and extra-curricular activities—extra-curricular as in raising sheep for various fairs, FFA, and school or 4-H fundraisers.

The minimal free time I had during the week I spent watching *Days of Our Lives*. I religiously recorded the daily showings on an old school VHS tape, the most advanced recording system of the era. Go ahead, laugh all you want, but my daily dose of *Days* paid off when the grand opening of Target in my home-town collided with my intimate relationship with the soap opera. On one hotter than s**t Saturday afternoon, Becky, one of my old aides and now good friend, called and asked my mom to take me to meet her and a few of my best buds at Target. Little did I know I was about to meet Robert Kellker-Kelly, better known as Bo Brady, the most well-known heartthrob on daytime television.

As Becky and I, along with my friends, all stood in line on the side of the newly opened Target building in 100-degree heat to see and get an autograph from "Bo Brady," what my friends called "the best surprise, ever" happened. I didn't know until after the fact, but someone had told "Bo" that there was a "poor little girl in a wheelchair out in the hot sun waiting to meet him." Okay, maybe it wasn't said just like that, but, whatever was said, well, it seems he wasn't having it, and I, with my entourage, were pulled from the line and ushered up, not to the front of the line, but smack-dab into the corded-off area in front of the man's face. My parents would have called that taking advantage of my resources. My friends called it being lucky. I called it "being disabled isn't all bad," especially because I was the first one, probably in the world, to learn and confirm my suspicions that Princess Gina was really Hope Brady. Now it sounds silly, but at that time in my life having inside information on the most watched day-time soap opera was like an OMG moment of today.

Anyway, back to the recording of TV programs. In those olden days, I had a television/VCR combination that I was able to operate without . . .mostly . . .any help, although my furniture paid the highest price for my independence because of the close proximity I had to get to the TV, many times which I grossly misjudged. I say mostly because twice a year I needed help changing the program settings. I knew how; I just wasn't fast enough to hit all the buttons in succession in what the TV system considered a timely fashion. After my first attempt at frustratingly resetting the clock on the TV so I could record *'Days'* at the correct hour of the day I conceded to needing and accepting help from someone. It is just one of those 'know when to fold 'em' kind of scenarios. Y'know, give in, call it quits, and ask for help. To be totally honest, my mom, to this day still needs help setting TVs, my wheelchair clock, and what have you. She has the physical dexterity but not the know-how. I have the know-how but not the physical dexterity.

    The shift in focus from home to school, as I mentioned before, was initiated as a two-part approach by my parents. As long as I can remember, my dad had always told my siblings and me that, "Everyone has a job in life, and right now your job is school. Your payment for doing that job is your "good" grades which will buy you things in the future. In other words, more simply put, the better your grades now, the more likely you are to make "big bank" later. The better your grades, the better off you are. So you need to do this job, this school thing, to the best of your ability so you will have more opportunity afforded to you later." He may have come up with that philosophy from knowing someone (wink, wink) who failed to be accepted into grad school due to (his) not up to par grades and a lower than desirable GPA.

    My mother's thoughts added to that philosophy. She felt and stated, many years later, that if my siblings and I were too busy and tired from school and after school activities then we'd be too tired to get into trouble. She strategically and continually implemented that idea throughout our academic careers up until college, keeping us far too busy, now that I think about it. Lucky for her it pretty much worked. My sister, brother, and I began to cherish "sleep-in Saturdays," and naps were an extra special treat.

One change I initially resisted and had a hard time accepting when I joined the ranks of elevated education during my first year of high school was the lack of attention paid to making it all about me. Well, not so much about me, per say, but making room for me, making all things possible and achievable. Suddenly, here in high school, met by new-to-me-students and teachers, I became aware and understood that continuing with such a mind-set, believing I was the center of all things, was neither realistic nor reasonable.

Now I'm not saying that I wasn't included, because I so was, just not in the same way as I was accustomed to being included. Up until this point, it was about making a place, room for me in every and all activities. It was about making me feel the same as everyone else. But the reality of life is that I was and am not like everyone else, just like everyone else is also not like everyone else . . .if that makes sense.

Let me give you a couple of examples of what I'm talking about. Initiation into the FFA organization required first-year members to memorize and recite the five paragraph FFA Creed. Since I have a memory like six elephants, it was a snap for me to complete that task—not so much so for other first-year members with far less-honed memories.

On the other hand, when it came time for Parliamentary Procedures or Opening and Closing competitions, I was told that I would be unable to participate on a team. I was obviously pissed as hell! I had never been excluded from an activity, ever, in my life! Yes, lots of times, okay, maybe most times, adaptations had to be made "for me" to be included. Denial of my participation was a new concept for me and difficult to wrap my head around. I did come to understand, however . . .and here is the reality of life, for anyone, really . . .that my non-participation wasn't because they, the advisors and students, didn't want me to participate nor because I didn't know procedures, terminology, or proper responses, because I did and still do to this day, mind you. It was because I would bring the team's score down solely because I was unable to participate physically: physically—as in an intricate part of the competition presentation of standing-up and sitting-down at appropriate times and points of interaction. I, of course, knew when all of those times existed: I just couldn't do them, the physical movements. Interestingly enough, though, having the previously mentioned knowledge of procedures, terminology, responses, and so forth, I was able to help from behind the scenes as a peer coach for our teams, and therefore was included "differently." Here no adaptation was ever made. I was able to contribute solely with what I had and could offer the teams.

It was because of those experiences— those experiences of exclusion, I guess you'd call it—that I truly learned that even though there were some things I just could not do, and that allowing me to do them only hurt the group as a whole, there was a plethora of things I could do that others could not that, in my "different-ness," enabled me to add to the group's success in my own way. Not only could I do things others couldn't, but, in reference to, for example, such things as caring for, exercising, and showing FFA animals, I did my part, in my own way, as well.

What am I trying to say? I'm trying to say that my fellow FFA peeps never let me "just have it." They focused on what I could do and not what I couldn't, and that is what I did . . .what I could do. We worked as a sort of community, taking advantage of each other's strengths or abilities. My strength was exercising pigs and lead-breaking and exercising sheep.

I can almost hear you giggle . . .exercising pigs! Yep, when you raise pigs and sheep, or any animal, for that matter, for show, they must be in prime condition, sort of like an athlete. As a group we figured out that tying the sheep to my wheelchair not only exercised them but also broke them to lead easily. Then someone had a lightbulb moment and turned the pigs out for me to herd around while leading the sheep. While I exercised everyone's animals, they in turn cleaned my pen and prepared feed for my animals. It was a definite win-win situation for everyone.

Referring back to my dad and his philosophy about everyone having jobs and doing the best job possible totally relates here. I was the best option for the job at hand. I was doing my part, my way, and in the process we were focusing on what I could do and taking advantage of that. In fact, my peers and I discovered being different was not only okay but absolutely advantageous. I mean, who else in the group could pull half-a-dozen sheep at a time while chasing ten or so pigs around an arena . . .all at one time. Nobody but me.

There were a couple of times I recall when I was like everyone else . . . and treated as such. I have to preface this with TEENAGE GIRLS ARE STUPID!!!!! In *Little Diva On Wheels,* I mentioned my very first best friend, Mary. As well, I mentioned, I guess you'd call it, my first and continual crush, Andrew. Can you guess where this is going? We were all friends during grade and middle school, that is, until those crazy female hormones began to make an appearance. Mary, even knowing of my feelings for Andrew, or maybe because of it, threw our friendship under the bus and, I felt, relentlessly pursued and claimed Andrew as her boyfriend. When I found out, she not only rubbed my nose it in, that she stole him away from me, but she laughed in my face . . .friendship over. The funny thing is

Andrew and I were never not friends, even while he and Mary were an item. End result: twenty something years later, teenage stupidity has gone by the wayside, and we are all older, wiser people, laughing at and remembering our past as friends—something we most often do now on Facebook as Facebook friends.

Another incident that sticks in my mind happened a few years later when I was a senior and barn-foreman at the school barn. It happened over a weekend when I decided to move the school's breeding sheep into pens that had never been used for sheep. In my defense, I thought I had a legitimate reason for the move. The beef pens, the spot where I moved the sheep to, were closer to the pasture, and therefore it was a shorter distance for me to herd the sheep out in the morning and back-in in the evening.

I'm not going to mention that I totally disregarded the fully enclosed ally-way that ran the entire distance of the whole frickin' barn behind all of the pens—sheep, beef, pigs . . .whatever—an ally-way entirely enclosed: as in the sheep couldn't go anyplace but to their designated area in less than three point two seconds. Come to find out there never was a problem in the first place, but boy, did I create one.

Anyway, come Monday afternoon the wrath of Mrs. Kerlee, the Ag Teacher, came raining down upon me. Sometime during the day, she had made her way to the school barn, like she did every day and found my "re-organization of livestock." At the time, I did not understand why, but she was NOT HAPPY with my unilaterally made decision. She blasted me like she would have blasted any other student who had done something she was not pleased with. She didn't just scold me, though; she explained why each species of animal had its own designated area in the barn. It was an effort to prevent cross contamination of diseases between species. Had I run my plan by her first, like I should have, she would have explained that to me. Towards the end of her rant, I'll call it, she got an "Oh, shit" look on her face as she remembered that my mother was standing a few feet away listening and watching the whole thing play out.

As Mrs. Kerlee looked up at my mother with a deer in the head-lights expression on her face, my mother said, "Don't stop on my account. If she did wrong, then she did wrong."

"But I forgot who she was. I forgot she was disabled, and I was treating her like I would any other kid." Mrs. Kerlee answered.

"And there is a problem with that?" My mother returned.

"But she's Jenni!" Mrs. Kerlee replied.

"So . . .remember when she was practicing for the Creed competition with the rest of the freshmen? Everyone directed their questions for Jenni to you. From the get-go, it only took you a time or two for you to say "TALK TO JENNI, not me. You need to address her like you would any other student," she reminded Mrs. Kerlee. "No difference here and now," my mother added.

Actually, Mrs. Kerlee pretty much always treated me like any other normal kid. I remember going to Regional Best Informed Greenhand Competition in San Luis Obispo. I had placed in the top three in both the Chapter and Sectional levels of competition, which allowed me to go on to the Regional level where FFA members from all over California competed. We're talking full dress uniform, black dress shoes, and hair (for us girls) up, neat, and off the collar. We didn't ever get out of the van until jackets were zipped and scarves in place. A little diva-ish . . .maybe, okay, yes, but it was because of our, dare I say, impeccable unified presentation at every competition or FFA event that we attended. We were dubbed, due to our can't be beat, possibly class act attitude and appearance, "The Hollister Bitches" early on. I'd rather call our diva . . .ish attitude us just being proud. I have to add that as a rule we won more often than not which also added to the "nickname."

How did I become aware of this nickname? It was at the above mentioned competition that my mom, who, as always, drove a group of us girls, in our van, overheard a comment soon after our feet, or wheels, in my case, hit the pavement. Her job or participation, or whatever you would like to call it, in any FFA event being complete, she generally took to the side lines and handed me my independence to do what I came to do. I didn't have a clue until we stopped for dinner on the way home that my mom had a story to share.

"So," she began. "You guys had a rough day."

"We know. Why are you reminding us?" One of the girls answered.

"Well, because while I was being *incognito*, I overheard more than one conversation about you guys."

"What!" We all screamed in unison. "Who? What did they say? Are you kidding?!"

"Not kidding," Mom answered. "But, really, I think what I heard was a complement in disguise."

We all looked at my mother totally confused, waiting for her to explain. "After I parked the van and was walking up toward the conference building, I heard several groups of kids from other FFA chapters or sections say, "Oh, Great! There Are The Hollister Bitches! We're Never Going To Win Now!"

"You can't be serious," I stammered, expressing what the others were thinking.

"Totally serious," Mom chuckled. "I believe you guys are somewhat intimidating to your competitors."

"Not today, that's for sure," someone else interjected. "We pretty much all sucked today."

Yep, that day we didn't even stay for the awards ceremony, which usually was a requirement set by Mrs. Kerlee. We all bombed . . .terribly. On the way home we pulled out every study guide, FFA manual, and guide book we had, to figure out what had happened. It basically boiled down to the fact that we studied the wrong part of EVERYTHING. Even Mrs. Kerlee, since she was able to accompany me into my testing room, didn't know the answers to the "off the wall" questions, as she called them.

Why do I bring this up? Why share my failure? Because I failed right alongside all of my fellow FFA members. In my mind, that is when you know you are truly part of a group. You see, being part of a group, a part of a whole, although a positive and desired station in life, is not always going to be butterflies and roses. Not all experiences are going to be positive, not a given, and failure is always an option, a possibility. So together we shared in our misery of loss and defeat only to fondly remember that day, years later, as the day we became the infamous and feared "Hollister Bitches" the one and only time we experienced an epic failure.

I also have to add here that during none of the competitions I entered was I ever given a break—with the exception of Mrs. Kerlee accompanying me into the exam room for the sole purpose of translating my verbal responses . . . .a service which, I am proud to say, I never used.

On the flip-side, being a member of a group definitely became evident to me on the day I rolled into Mr. Homen's senior government class where we all had to learn, memorize, and recite the preamble to the United States Constitution in front of the whole class. (I know, out of timely order, but it's when the memory hit me in relation to group vs. individual accomplishments, so bear with me once again.) I knew I wanted to be the first to recite it and get it over with. Years earlier, while fiddle-farting around not wanting anything to do with math, math homework, or any kind of numbers, period, my mom gave me some pretty sage and savvy advice even a third grader could understand. She said, "If you get to it and do it right the first time, you only have to do it once and not think about it again." Still good advice today.

So anyway, I made my desire known to Mr. Homen and was immediately shut down. You have to understand that he had been a teacher for somewhere around a bazillion years and had his own way of doing things, a way he thought was fair—which in reality it was. Mr. Homen had an orange pill bottle full of little pieces of paper with numbers on them from one to however many students were in the class. Each student pulled a number from the bottle and that was the order in which we would recite the preamble. Although I had an aide in class with me, Mr. Homen insisted on pulling my number for me since my fine motor manual dexterity is basically non-existent. Low and behold, what number did he pull? You guessed it . . .number 1. The look he gave me was utter surprise and amazement. Then he asked if I was ready, now. I told him that I came in ready.

So off I went without pause. I do remember him being able to make it to his desk before I began, though. I successfully recited the whole preamble in one smooth delivery with no mistakes. Mr. Homen only made two comments. The first, "I'm not surprised, Jenni. You did an expected great job." The second was to the rest of the class. "If Jenni was able to do that well, you guys have a lot to live up to and should be able to do at least as well."

It was a few days later, after the last student in my class had successfully recited the preamble, without error, that Mr. Homen informed us that out of all of his United States Government class he had that year this one was the only one in which 100% of the class delivered the preamble, in his words, "Perfectly."

Now that I look back at it, I want to say I was the reason. A little arrogant? Maybe. But I believe I was the impetus for the class' accomplishment, for their having to strive to be as good as me, the disabled girl who could throw a challenge down and put a bee in anybody's bonnet. Kind of a bold and presumptuous statement in a poor-me-kind-of-way, I know, but having lived a "few" more years since then and studying human nature as we all do, I believe they didn't want to be less than the disabled girl.

I suppose I threw down the gauntlet, and they picked it up and ran. I guess what I am trying to say is that me, having the ability to memorize like a freaking elephant, pushed the rest to their own reachable perfection.

Interestingly, a couple of weeks later, after settling in to watch a movie about the inner workings of the White House (which opened with the recital of the preamble), the entire class, unrehearsed and unprompted, joined in, adding our voices to that of the movie's voice flawlessly. We were the only class to do so. Mr. Homen was impressed. He said as much when the movie ended. This is just one example of how, even with my less than perfect individuality, we, the United States Government class, developed a kind of imperfect comradery of perfection.

I just realized that I haven't mentioned one of the most important people, friend, and confidant absolutely known to mankind. She became almost a family member. I spent more of my waking hours with her than I did my parents and siblings during my high-school years. Her name is Debbie, and she was my one-on-one aide during all four years of high-school. We actually met years earlier when I was in pre-school. Talk about the six-degrees of Kevin Bacon. I'm going to go way back here for a second. My special-education preschool teacher was a woman whose name was Madeline, who was friends with a woman named Vee, a special-education aide, who popped in and out of my classroom to help on occasion. Vee (her real name is Vera, but she hates it, so she goes by Vee) was (and still is) best friends with Debbie, another special-education aide. While Madeline was setting up one of our infamous school overnight camping trips, she asked Vee if she had any suggestions as far as more staffing for the camping trip. Before I go any further, here is a visual to give you a full understanding of the awesomeness of these special education folks and community that I was lucky enough to be involved with and supported by, from pre-school all the way through high-school.

Imagine, if you will (and I say this with the utmost friendship, love and, yes, support that I shared with each and every one of those classmates, the imperfect bunch that we were) supervising and keeping corralled a couple-three-dozen; deaf, blind, mute, autistic, ADHD, self-harming, mentally and physically disabled, Downs Syndrome, disfigured, behaviorally uncontrollable, and the list goes on, children. I may have missed a few conditions or dysfunctions or disabilities, but you get the idea.

Let's start out with the common knowledge that being a teacher for so called "normal" students is a hard enough job as it is. Now, add to that attempting to meet the needs of each individual special-needs child. Piece of cake . . .right? But before you get started you have to set aside any academic goals that may have popped into your head because that ain't happenin'. Most are still working on life skills like brushing their teeth or using the bathroom . . .ya, appropriate for some. I'd kind of like to compare the Special Ed. classroom to attempting to juggling in a circus while tight-rope walking for the first time, without a net. Finally, dump all that into the wide-open, uncontained, uncontrolled, swimming-pool filled, rough terrain, fire-pitted, with marshmallow roasting sticks wilderness. Doesn't sound so easy-peasy now, does it?

While doing research for this book, I found what I thought might be a helpful resource for anyone needing or looking into Special Education Services for Preschoolers with Disabilities for their child, and I wanted to share, so here it is: https://www.parentcenterhub.org/preschoolers/.

    Anyway, back to my story. Vee volunteered herself and her bestie, Debbie. Once we got to the campsite, my dad and I were introduced to Debbie. After the camping trip, I really never saw her again, or I didn't think I did, until I happened to be outside of my freshman high-school summer school math class with a short-term aide named Kathy. I was attempting to get my math requirement out of the way so I had more room in my schedule for things like Ag class . . .and math sucks, so taking it during the summer as my only class gave me the time and opportunity to concentrate all my efforts on that one and only subject, 'cause I hated it. Debbie, of course, remembered me, that cute little blonde-haired three-or-four-year old from the camping trip. I didn't know until we started talking that Debbie had been on the fringes of and keeping track of me and my scholastic career since that first camping trip. It seems as though being involved in the special education community is like being caught in a spider web that you are unable to escape. Once you are in, you are in. And from my freshman year of high-school on, Debbie was in it with me.

The simplest way for me to explain my four years of high-school with Debbie would best be represented by her determination to make room for me, making all things possible and achievable (something I earlier referenced as not being realistic) or at least within my capabilities, interests, and desires. A lot of times she was out of her zone of comfort or knowledge, but that didn't stand in our way. Debbie wasn't necessarily a city girl, but a farm/ranch girl she was not. She had a lot to learn about agriculture, especially my sheep, and she was always up for the challenge. (Funny memory just came to me . . .Debbie always marveled that her hands always felt so soft and smooth so quickly after handling the dirty, skanky sheep. I remember asking or testing her on the contents of hand lotion and where she thought it, the lanolin, came from. It was a true light bulb moment for her!

Recently, as I always do when I mention someone in a book, I emailed Debbie for her permission to do so. I just had to include a portion of her reply. These are her words:

> I tell stories about how you and I went thru so many fun adventures during our four years together at school. From us both getting into trouble for laughing in class, so much so that Mr. Ackerman threatened to throw us out (I truly believed deep down he found it humorous as we were not the trouble type), to learning

with sparks flashing to arc weld in Mrs. Kerlee's class (and remember when we were tig welding and my arm started to get hot only to find the kid next to us had the rod touching my shirt and burnt a hole in it, to me learning how you castrate a poor little lamb with a rubber band!!!!! You really put me through the hoops, Jennifer Kuhns, (and I loved every moment of it)!

One of my biggest light-bulb moments came when she and I were in the gas-welding booth during Ag class. Had my mother only known . . .Okay, here is the set-up. The rest of the class was arc-welding—which, if you don't know, runs at about 6,000 degrees, whereas gas is "only" about 3,600 degrees. Mrs. Kerlee, the ag teacher, and Debbie had previously discussed the level of comfort Debbie had while me-and-she were, literally, playing with fire. All things considered, the lower temperature, quicker shut-off ability, less concentration of heat . . .la-la-la . . .and so forth, led Debbie to believe that we could get it done. I was stoked about giving it a shot. Who doesn't like to play with fire . . .if only once? Such a Silly Lady. Remember me? *spastic* quadriplegic . . .(No one was hurt in the resurrection of this memory.)

Actually, one of our first, mine and Debbie's, brilliant ideas to assimilate or integrate me into high-school life, or whatever you want to call it, was an epic fail. After much discussion between the two of us during my first P.E. class, we developed a plan. The plan was based upon total inclusive participation, and for total participation I needed . . .you guessed it . . .clothes. This time P.E. clothes, as ugly as they were, I needed (no, I just wanted) them and having the opportunity to shop was an added bonus. What was I thinking, right? The rest of the, I have to say, well thought out plan was to change into said red shorts and white tee-shirt with the school's name written across the front before class. Since it was my last class for the day, I would wear them home and not have to change again.

On day one of P.E. I was decked out with the rest of my class in the red and white uniform. Problem one, it took Debbie much, much longer to get me out of the chair, my clothes off, and the damn, not so cute after all, shorts and tee-shirt on than anyone else. This brought up problem two, which was the fact that I was no longer a one-person lift, and another person had to be brought in to help Debbie. Such a waste of time, resources, and energy. This of course brings us to REALITY and problem number three! How much was I or did I actually do or think I was going to do in P.E. that I needed to change into different clothes? Not that I have to remind you, but wheelchair bound, spastic quadriplegic cerebral palsy here! Realistically and logistically my physical participation was never going to be a "thing." But my classmates, once again, were able to see beyond that and gave me a job I was best suited for that enabled me to support them at the same time. And what was that? Well, did I mention I have a better than average memory? I kept score and called rule violations. Since I read and memorized the rules and regulations of each sport they played, etc., I knew them by heart. They seemed to understand that "I don't have to be what you are," to be. Looking back, this kind of reinforces my thoughts and feelings, my belief that children left to their own devices are generally wonderful creations! I became aware through my experiences, my life, that it isn't until adult involvement, infusion of their thoughts, opinions and prejudices, that that changes.

Those same classmates, on October 27, 1994, not only showed, but proved their understanding and acceptance of me by nominating me for Freshman Homecoming Princess. I didn't win, but I have to say that I felt immensely honored to have been nominated by those whom I held in the highest regard. But more than that, I felt truly accepted by the masses, by my classmates, because they chose me to represent them as a whole, with me as part of that whole.

Although physical education was not my forte, one subject that I fell more in love with as a freshman was English literature. I had always loved the subject, but here I was immersed into the virtuosity of symbolism in writing. Here was my safe "on-fire" place, a place, a thing I was good at, a talent I had that I didn't need help with, except to turn the pages of the book. (Fast forward twenty years or so and that problem has taken care of itself with the one in every household Kindle and an Audible account.)

Here's a little brag: I had such a skill for finding—and explaining—symbolism, my teacher basically appointed me as the "go-to" for my contemporaries when they needed help or explanation. I fast became known among my peers for my ability to dissect literature in any form and spent many hours explaining the meaning of such things as "ten white pigs," the title of the short story "The Yellow Wallpaper," and "a three-legged stool." The three-legged stool, for example, can mean two things: either the Father, the Son, and the Holy Spirit or the past, the present, and the future. I may not be able to play with fire or sing worth a damn, but I'm still a Symbolism Diva.

I said I had a skill for explaining symbolism. I suppose there is a proviso to that statement, a disclaimer, so to speak. One of the complications attributed to cerebral palsy, for me, anyway, affects speech. Trust me, I can speak—loud, but not so clear. I've always had an advanced vocabulary, but this is how it breaks down. I see a word; I can spell the word, define the word, use the word appropriately, and I can say the word. The problem is "saying" and "enunciating" a word are two absolutely, completely, different animals. I explained more thoroughly in *Little Diva On Wheels* how speech can be affected by cerebral palsy, and let me tell you, affected I was, or I should really say am, 'cause some things just don't change.

All that being explained, you know how little kids often have imaginary friends they speak to and play with and how the old television show *Ghost Whisperer* told the viewer that all children can see ghosts until they grow up and no longer believe? The premise of the show was that they, the children, no longer believe because of the adult formation of things like inhibitions, logic, reserve, and such. Stay with me here. I'm really not a lunatic. I'm trying to lay ground-work for an observed theory, insane as it might sound. My theory, my point, is that children are always more accepting and open-minded than adults. Why am I bringing this up? Because I felt the need to address my verbal shortcomings while giving my peers major kudos for always understanding what I have come to call my CP-babblelistics. And this is in contrast to most adults who don't even pretend or attempt to put forth any effort whatsoever into trying to understand me and my less than perfect verbiage.

Don't get me wrong. I am not against or trying to bash adults. I am one. If you noticed, I said most adults. I have found over the years three groups of adults that do understand my CP-babblelistics. One is "most" family members, and I have to emphasis "most" because . . .well . . .because some just don't. I'd like to chalk it up to those being too logical-minded or impatient or . . .okay, I don't really know, but I had to throw something out here, a hypothesis of sorts.

The second group is close friends or people who have been around me for, let's just say a while. These folks, for example, are like my friend, also named Jennifer. She was a 4-H and FFA friend—actually more than a friend, but anyway, I have known her since I was nine-years-old. One day her mother, who I had also known since I was nine, came to me with all kinds of questions about being disabled. She was a teacher and was taking extended education classes in which she was researching and writing a paper on disabilities and the difficulties that we disabled people are faced with every day. It was a long time ago, but I remember the short and sweet conversation Jennifer had with her mother, via Jennifer's mother, after the fact. It went something like this.

Jennifer's mother, after she had blindfolded herself for a day and tied her thumbs down so she couldn't use them for another day (so she could, herself, experience "being" disabled), verbalized her idea to Jennifer. "I want to talk to Jenni about being disabled to get her perspective."

Jennifer's response was pretty much priceless. "Why would you want to talk to her? She isn't disabled."

"Jennifer," her mother countered, "a . . .wheelchair?!?"

"Oh, yeah," Jennifer responded. "I forgot."

And there you have it. When someone can forget or not see a five- hundred-pound wheelchair when they look at a person, that is probably the most sought-after reaction (or lack thereof) that any physically disabled person wishes for. See Me!

Now on to group three. I have a ton of fun with this group. Group three is inclusive of all the people who either have a family member, a friend, someone they work with, or for some other reason have had extensive personal interaction with someone disabled. I tend to appreciate this fine bunch of people a lot, although it took me a bit of time to put two together and figure out why these people stood-out for me. These were, initially, not friends or family members, but mere acquaintances. Even so, each and every time I ran across a member of this group, I was treated—dare I say it—like a human-being. I was greeted, not ignored. I was spoken to, not at. I was not made to feel like I had leprosy. And I was verbally understood. Now, and for many years, I can almost always and instantly tell when I meet a member of this wonderful group because they are not afraid or leery of me. When I ask them who they know who is disabled, I always get the same shocked look of 'How do you know?,' like I have extra-sensory perception. 'Nope,' my simple answer is, 'you aren't afraid of me.'

But it is crazily interesting and annoying how . . .how what? . . .how friggin' closed-minded and just flat-out afraid of things most adults are of people, circumstances, and situations that are different or beyond their comfort-zone or comprehension.

This brings me to my grandfather, a wonderful, supportive, loving, giving—there are so many more adjectives I could use to describe this man—but . . .for most of his life he could never understand anything I ever said. So, for my grandfather—after having a fairly significant stroke—to lose his _in_ability to understand me was way intriguing. Yes, I said inability, as in he was unable to understand a single word I uttered until after his stroke. It was weird, weird; it was just weird!

Let me explain. As people do, we went to visit him in the hospital following the stroke. Conversations were going on between and among multiple people in his room. Kind of out of the blue, thinking back on it now, I'm betting he wanted to involve me in the conversational banter (because that's who he was). He turned to me and said something to the effect of not wanting to be in the hospital and that physical therapy really, really sucked. I answered him with one of his own favorite lines. "Grandpa, you are preaching to the choir." To my complete and utter—not to mention the rest of the occupants of the room's—amazement, he answered me. No, I mean he answered me with an answer that was an appropriate answer for the answer I gave him about therapy sucking. From that day forward he was able to understand every single word I spoke.

It goes without saying that the stroke changed my grandfather's brain-chemistry due to portions of brain-death. You also have to understand that the man could, prior to his stroke, add a column of ten six-digit numbers in his head (faster than a calculator, mind you). Following his stroke, he could no longer even take a walk around his own neighborhood without forgetting where he lived or knowing how to get home by himself.

Now if I was a philosophy major or something like that, I would theorize, with a little eerie, maybe creepy twist (as in the case of the children and ghost thing I mentioned before), that, with the death of part of my grandfather's brain, he seemed to have lost his adult inhibitions and reticence. Wow . . .hang on here . . .I just had a bit of an epiphany, why it seemed important to me to babble on about this. I'm kind of talking about myself here. There may have been different causes but basically the same result: Brain-Death. We, more or less, became kindred souls. The only difference is his loss was cognitive while mine is physical.

In his instance, I'm prone to think, his loss of some of his cognitive function caused comfort-zone changes. He was no longer so closed-minded but, instead, more accepting of things most adults are afraid of. His circumstances and situations were altered, and, therefore, I'd say, philosophically speaking—like I know what I'm talking about—so was his comprehension and mindset. Simpler said . . .it takes one to know one.

Speaking of taking one to know one, I have to share my competitive nature and how it and adult/parent intervention can ruin good friendships. I'm going to give you my best example of what I am talking about. Prior to high-school and throughout high-school, as I mentioned in *Little Diva On Wheels,* I was not only mentored by my friend Matt Perkins, whose knowledge of all things sheep surpassed his years, I was also encouraged and supported by, well . ..basically by the entire county. All the other Ag kids and I were good friends, competitive in the show ring with an extreme attitude of fairness. On the outside of the ring we helped each other and shared knowledge. The tickler when showing animals at a fair is the rules, regulations, and stipulations. What am I talking about? The biggie and probably the most tested and complained about "rule" was "No adult assistance or help with any animal once on the fairground premises." I know, sounds doable, like a no-brainer. I'm not talking about me, by the way, I'm talking about that first year nine-year-old 4-H kid that weighs, maybe, seventy-five pounds lifting their 125-pound lamb up onto the blocking table that is around two feet off the ground. And let's get real here! How many of those sheep, pigs, or steers were fed, groomed, lead-broke, or in some other fashion, taken care of by mom and dad at home? Oh, and who is hauling said animal to the fairgrounds in whose vehicle? Sorry, this rant over . . .but it is a sore spot for me.

    Getting back to my original point: rules, friends, fairness, and adult interference. Having known about the "no hands on" rule for adults since I was nine-years-old, I had a laminated letter from the fair administration stating that I could, in fact, have adult help. That letter was on my person at all times as well as on file in the fair office for anyone to check—'cause I could have made the whole thing up or forged signatures, which believe it or not, I was accused of. Anyway, the thought was that the physical help, paired with my knowledge and instruction to said helper, would place me on equal ground in my participation with my peers.

So here is where the adult influences came into play and pretty much ruined everything. As a new FFA member, I became acquainted with a new group of people. These people were deeply immersed in the world of livestock and competitions, as was my friend Matt's family. When I first met the kids, they were great! They were friends; they were helpful; we were classmates; they were fun to be around—supportive, uplifting . . .We sometimes fed their animals for them when they were out of town, and they did the same for me. They funny thing was, they knew I was raising sheep to show at our county fair right alongside and against them. They, the girls, had NO PROBLEM with the concept of competition! Now you have to understand that these girls were what are called "show jocks." Their life pretty much revolved around breeding and showing animals. And of course, every parent wants their child to do and be the best. That is where, surprisingly, "I" became an interference. I say surprisingly, because it was a surprise to the girls' parents that I was, apparently, a force to be reckoned with and might just knock them out of the winner circle.

Those parents, those adults, bitched, complained, fussed, and fumed to fair officials and/or anyone else who would listen to their claim of injustice because, in their minds, there was no way I could possibly have the intelligence or skill set to raise the caliber of animal I seemed to have raised. The stupid thing was, they weren't griping about who did what to or for the animals at home all the months prior to the fair, the actual feeding, watering, exercising, grooming, the actual growing and raising of the animal. They were griping about who was going to feed, take the blanket off, card (as in comb), polish hooves, and help show . . .for the one day at the fair.

On top of all that, when the parents found out that it wasn't actually my parents who were helping fit (get the lamb groomed and ready) and show my animal, but Matt Perkins, they hollered FOUL again because FOR GOD'S SAKE he's A SHOW JOCK! Yep, he was not only one of them, a show jock, but one of the best of them. There is this saying that goes something like this, "When you are good, you are bad. Matt was very, very bad, and I had the great fortune to be mentored by and friends with that number one badass.

I have always believed that discrimination and prejudice is a learned behavior. Prior to that first fair, the girls and

I were, I'd like to think, good friends. After the ranting and raving of their parents, who I truly think were jealous of someone else's accomplishments above their own while living vicariously through their children and "who I had been aligned with," we were shoved back into being mere polite acquaintances. In my opinion, it isn't until adult involvement—infusion of their thoughts, opinions, and prejudices—that relationships are forced to change, usually not for the better.

It has been brought to my attention, over the years, that I have a really strange sense of humor. I like to play, sometimes, not on the positive but on the negative for a laugh or, at least, for my own entertainment. Actually, early on I learned to address the negatives, my negatives, about me and my disability and poke fun at myself before others could poke it at me. It kind of stops people in their tracks. That is exactly what I did when I overheard friends of the above mentioned "show jock" girls' family. <u>I started a rumor</u>, a false rumor, mind you, but a rumor all the same. Why, you might ask. I don't know why. Entertainment, like I said, I guess . . .no, I really wanted to stir the crap. I wanted to see how fast the rumor would get around and to whom.

What was the rumor, and how did I get it started? While having lunch at a local pizza parlor with my mom and grandmother, in walks a woman who was one of the girls' family friends. (It would be so much easier if I used names, but slander and all that . . .) My mother and I knew her as well, but none of us acknowledged each other because, frankly, because my connection with Matt interfered with their high and mighty plans for the girls. It seems I had become threatening. On our side, she and her husband were well known in the county for . . .how should I put this . . .shenanigans, and no one, or people I held in high and fair regard, wanted to be associated with them because of their . . .hummm . . .let's just say, because of their questionable practices. Not to mention the fact they were front and center in the small group of parents that tried to ban me from exhibiting my animals. Not my favorite people, to say the least.

There I go again, getting all off-topic, but background is needed to set the stage, so to speak. The rumor . . .the rumor was that I bought a "ringer" lamb (Ya'll know what a ringer is, right? . . .Okay . . .it's a $1000 lamb.) and had Matt bring it back from the biggest sheep-breeding operation in Colorado. That was how the spoken-too-loudly, on-purpose, overheard-conversation went.

I initially whispered to my mom and grandmother, "Just go with me here."

"Hey, Grandma, I just got my fair lamb."

Grandma jumped right in with, "Oh yeah, where did you get it from?"

"Matt just brought it back for me from 'that' big sheep ranch in Colorado."

My grandmother exclaimed, "Wow, you are getting real about this, aren't you?"

And that is when someone's ears sitting at a table a short distance away perked up and couldn't get close enough to our table. There was some serious leaning going on.

Now, I have to admit, all that was true. I bought a lamb from people Matt knew in Colorado, and he picked it up for me, along with one for himself, and brought them home. In my opinion, the best rumors begin with a grain of truth delivered in an overly-entitled manner, as any Diva would do, followed by a flat-ass, are-you-kidding-me? lie.

This is where my mother interjected, "Yes, she is," with a smirky look at me, then added, "Tell her how much you shelled out for it."

Looking over my shoulder at the table with the looky-loos, I answered, "One-thousand bucks."

Totally aware of what was going on and having just gotten the go-for-it-nod from my mom, my grandmother chimed in, "That's a whole lot of money just to have the best lamb and win. I can see that your plan is to win at any cost, isn't it?"

"You bet it is!" I answered as I snuck another peek at the nearby table and its occupants who now had eyes as big as the pizza pan sitting in front of them. Okay, okay,

I flat-out lied. Not my proudest moment, but, GOD, IT WAS FUN . . .

You may not understand the significance of what I had just lied about. Let me explain. The purchase price of a market lamb back then averaged around $125.00 for a, roughly, forty to fifty-pound lamb. Then there is the added cost of feed, minimally around $100.00, bedding at $25.00, time, energy and effort raising, and so forth, for several months until said lamb reaches, let's say, 120 pounds. At which time, it gets shown and is sold through an auction scenario. Again, I'm talking about over twenty years ago when an average price for a market lamb was—and I'm being extremely generous here—$4.00 a pound. So do the math. A one-thousand, one-hundred and twenty-five calculable (minus time, energy, and manual labor) -dollar-output, opposed to a sale price of $480.00. I'm no math genius, but come on! That is friggin' ridiculous in my book.

But that isn't the funniest part. The hilariousness is in the fact that it took less than three days for the rumor to spread around the entire county and for parental visitors, not the kids, mind you, to show up at the school farm to see and ask questions for themselves about this "ringer" lamb I "supposedly" purchased. It was one of my greatest joys to ask them questions of my own, like "Who told you that?" which of course was never answered in a CYA attempt and "How stupid do you think I am?" The looks on their faces and stumbling mumbling was priceless. I'm still not sure any of them believed me because that lamb was DAMN GOOD!

Why am I harping on this animal thing? First of all, 4-H, FFA, and raising sheep were a huge part of my life from the age of nine through the end of high-school. It started as a "Let's give it a shot" kind of thing and blossomed and grew into, me, a girl with broken wings, a crippled kid in a wheelchair becoming a threat to some of the most competitive and experienced show jocks in, not only the county, but the show circuit. This little diva was undeniably a force to be reckoned with and taken seriously in and out of the show ring.

Secondly, I wanted to show that "it," whatever "it" is, can be done. I wanted to demonstrate that people with disabilities "can do" whatever they want, at least to some degree. Let's get real here. You have to admit that even able-bodied people can't always do "all" things with perfect or great efficiency.

Thirdly, and probably the most universal and normal aspiration of any child, is to be and do like Mom or Dad or some other family member they look up too. Now, obviously raising animals is an unlikely hobby or desire, but when you discover your mom had done the same and won something called Round Robin (the highest showmanship honor that exists) you want to shoot for the moon as well. It's kind of like that old Life Cereal commercial. *I want to be like Mikey . . .*

And I wanted to be so much like Mikey that I conned my mom into allowing me the opportunity to not only apply for but, against all common-sense or logic, be offered the position of FFA barn-foreman, a paid position, a job, a real job, one that included a variety of physical tasks such as sweeping, raking leaves, scrubbing out water-troughs, giving animal inoculations, breeding school-owned animals, delivering newborn animals (along with my own), and so much more, none of which I, obviously, could physically do.

The way I solved that problem? In discussions with my mother I convinced her to let me take the job with the caveat that she would be my hands, my legs, my back, my physical strength for which we negotiated payment for her services out of my paycheck. Yep, I was not only an employee, but I was also an employer.

You might think that the physical was the whole of the job and I was getting paid for doing nothing. Not true. My part of the deal, the job, was the cognitive, the cerebral part. (For me to use the word cerebral, as in palsy here, as in doesn't work, may sound weird to you, I know.)

What I'm trying to say is that my cognitive, my 'mental function' and capacity was and has always been absolutely fine. (Some might even call me a tad obsessive- compulsive because of the way I run scenarios with possible results through my head and the way I can move fluidly from plan A to plan B to plan C because you always need a backup to the backup). Anyway, my portion of the job was thought-based, while my mother's portion was based on the physical. I was the decision maker, the schedule preparer, the record keeper, the routine setter, the organizer and planner. Ultimately, I was the one held responsible for what did and didn't go down at the barn because the person really in charge, my Ag teacher, didn't care how things got done to her satisfaction, just that they got done to her satisfaction.

Remember that Ag Teacher who denied my participation in Opening and Closing Competitions for the good of the team, because of my physical limitations? She was the same Ag Teacher who gave me the job. After hearing my proposed plan, she fully believed in my capability to do the job better than any other applicant. By this point in time she had learned and appreciated my anal-retentive nature when it came to getting things done . . .somehow, some way.

Even though I spent way too many hours at the school barn during my high-school years, that was not my only interest. I had an academic and school social life outside of making sure animal enclosures were muck free.

One class and extracurricular activity I wished I could have participated in before my junior and senior years was journalism. That was the prerequisite: being at least a junior.

Let me take that back. A student could be in the actual class prior to their junior year but could not be part of the editorial staff, do interviews, or write actual articles. Nor could they make any decisions on what did or did not go into *The Baler*, the school paper.

Anyway, this was a major segue into what I do now. I write. I write children's books, most of which have a disabled protagonist with a strong and positive character and attitude. Well, maybe a little bit of a snarky attitude . . .What can I say?, I put a little bit of me into all of my characters.

This is, of course, absolutely diametrically opposed to how one, a newspaper reporter, should write. I learned early on that it is unethical to insert your own opinions, thoughts, and beliefs while reporting on the facts of an event. I have to say, this was an extremely difficult idea for me to wrap my head around. Why, because I had always been taught to express myself, make myself heard, and my needs known. To be a reporter I sort of had to unlearn the idea of injecting my own opinion into things—something that went against the grain of my whole being. And to tell you the truth, I wasn't sure, in the beginning that this journalism thing was going to work for me because I'm nothing if not opinionated.

Interjecting a funny story here, proving my opinionated nature, even as a very small child: the reason I'm including it at this juncture is because the story was recently retold by my mother to my grandmother whom the story is about.

So my grandmother and I were shopping together one day. I was probably eight or nine years old and still small enough for her to transfer me from a car seat to my fold-up manual wheelchair. I loved these shopping trips because I generally . . .no not generally . . .always came home with a plethora of items I did not need. On this particular trip, my grandmother was looking for a blouse for some special occasion. She found one she liked and held it up in front of herself under her chin and asked my opinion which I promptly gave. Keep in mind, she did ask.

My answer . . ."You can't wear that."

"Why?" she asked.

"Because it brings out the 'W' word."

"The what?" my grand- mother questioned confused.

"Y'know, the 'W' word, your WRINKLES!" Unabashedly, I laughed.

She bought the blouse anyway and has it to this very day. (Too funny, my mother just told me that my grandmother can't bear to get rid of it because of the memory and that she, my grandmother, plans to one-day gift me that blouse.)

Just when I was thinking I needed to switch directions and find a different, what I'd now call my passion, is when I was offered the features column alongside my good friend, Jennifer Geraci. To explain the difference, a good newspaper reporter reports the news as it is. A good features columnist possesses a keen sense of and ability for storytelling, and that was right up my alley. It wasn't too long before we became the co-features editors, and worked side by side for the school paper, overseeing all other features writers. (Kind of a side note here: Do you remember me mentioning my having a one-on-one aide, Debbie? Although she wasn't technically allowed to leave me alone and to my own devices, that is more or less how our time in journalism went. Jennifer G. and I were pretty much self-sufficient when it came to writing and/or editing our column. Because of that, Debbie spent those fifty-five minutes returning her own phone calls, writing notes, reading, and taking an occasional catnap.)

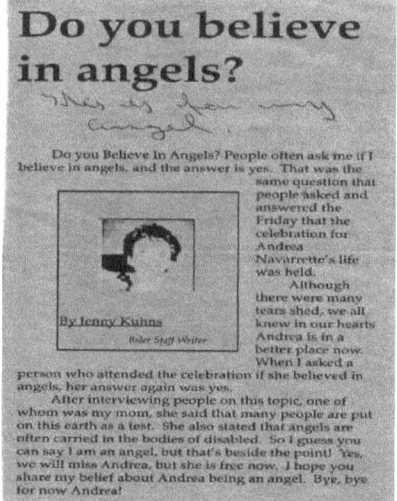

I don't know if I have mentioned it before now, but as a person with a physical disability, I quickly discovered that as a rule, as "my norm," I had and still continually have to work twice as hard as my peers, or anyone else for that matter, to even be considered an equal . . .and, and, and then be accused of being an over-achiever!!!!!! Once I earned my position and place on the editorial staff because of my abilities, that was no longer the case. I no longer had to prove myself. The staff knew what I could contribute and put me to task. However, the juxtaposition of having to work twice as hard to be equal—and then, at the same time, to be labeled an over-achiever—will always be an obstacle to overcome, at least for me. I have another story about this to share later on, one that happened a few years in the future from where we are now in my timeline. It was during my time at CSU Stanislaus when I was an undergraduate student working toward my Bachelor of Art degree. Just tuck that away for a bit.

I previously mentioned how my dad viewed school. School was our job, and my siblings and I were expected to do this job, school, to the best of our ability. To me this meant doing more than was required, hence, the working twice as hard, being a self-starter and over-achieving, I guess. Actually, to this day my siblings and I are tremendously competitive, which has overflowed to my nieces and nephew . . .a good or bad thing . . .I don't know, but it seems to push one to do their very best at whatever it is they want to do. My sister, just the other day, reminded me how we felt about winning second place at something, or anything, for that matter. It was never second best. It was and, if you want to know the truth, still is FIRST LOSER!

As a result, in my senior year government class, an assignment was given. All of Mr. Homen's government classes were to write a paper titled *My Voice in Our Democracy*. I didn't know it at the time, but Mr. Homen was searching for what he called the perfect paper to enter into the local V.F.W. sponsored speech contest of the same title. He only chose one paper out of all five of his U.S. government classes—mine—to submit to the contest. It was only after the fact that he found it 'appropriate' to inform me of his actions—only because I had won the local chapter contest and the V.F.W. wanted me to attend and read/give my speech at the regional contest level. Surprised and excited as I was, it was also at that time that I freaked out because aaaaa . . .babblelistics, and most adults' inability to understand me. Here we go again with making it work!

What was the plan? Mr. Homen approached one of my fellow classmates, Erica, and asked if she would be willing to read and record my speech on a cassette recorder for the next level of competition.

(That's how old I am. We had cassette recorders.) Easy peasy, right? But it was a difficult decision. 'Her' voice was not 'my' voice, but more likely than not, my voice would not be understood well enough to get 'my' message across. Ultimately, with cassette and recorder in hand, we, Mr. Homen, my mother, and I attended the regional speech competition where I was . . .you got it . . .First Loser. Many, believing my speech itself was better than the one that won, thought it would have been more profound and better received had I given my own speech. Maybe, maybe not. We'll never know. Decision's made.

That My Voice in Our Democracy experience still gave me a needed kick in the butt. Again I was reminded that it wasn't all about me. The speech contest was perfectly timed, just prior to the holidays, because I was still able to organize a community-service-based food drive. It may not have been my voice in democracy, but it was my way of giving back to a community that had supported me for so many years. Okay, maybe it was a little about me, too, because it fulfilled yet another one of Mr. Homen's government class requirements of doing some type of community service. This was something I came up with on my own and that I could do on a somewhat larger scale than writing an editorial on helping through the holidays or going to a pet shelter and petting dogs. And not to mention, I could do this 'somewhat . . .kind of, with only a driver and bag carrier' on my own. Oh, and BTW, my community service helped ALL my classmates, those who donated to my food drive, fulfill their community service requirements! Two birds with one stone you might say . . .or maybe three birds because again, Mr. Homen was impressed with my ingenuity and ability to get my friends and classmates to rally around my cause, my idea, and get it done.

 I am proud to say that this is something I not only still do, but it has become a family thing. For example, nieces and nephew donate toys— purchased with money they have saved all year, mind you—to Toys for Tots. Another would be just this last year, in November, during the Camp Fire, my aunt sent a check and asked my mother to "do something" with it for those who were in need. It has become a wonderful family tradition.

 You may be wondering why I am sharing all of these seemingly small and insignificant things, these stories, these positive pat-myself-on-the- back little moments, these snapshots of pride and perseverance. I'm sharing them because I want to show how a disabled person, a diva, if you will, with broken wings can still fly, can contribute to her or his world, in even the simplest of ways.

But at the same time I also need to be real. I need to fess up and be honest. In preparation for this book I read through some of my high-school journals and found this passage that I wrote in 1995. (Actually still being real, Debbie wrote it while I dictated.)

> ...Everyone says I'm pretty smart, FFA, taking care of eight head of sheep. The only catch is I'M TRAPPED in a quadriplegic body. Sometimes like now I feel like I have a body from HELL. People like Mom and Debbie try to pat me on the back and say "It's okay, it will be okay," but I'll be damned if it is going to be okay. Last night I went into my room and wanted to cry, but couldn't. I wanted to scream, but then my mom would come down the hall and ask why I was screaming.

I don't recall what my "poor-me" issue was at the time, but my point is, I had them at fifteen-years-old and before, and I still have them today a couple of decades later. I'm guessing up until this point I've portrayed or lead you to believe that my life was and is all up and happy, all butterflies and roses. Not so. Maybe more not so than most. I could feel sorry for myself with the best of them.

On the flip side, a couple of weeks later I (Debbie) wrote this:

> Talk about a crock of bull—I don't know what was wrong with me for the last couple of weeks. Whatever it was, it's gone: yeah! I guess what changed it was either Saturday or yesterday. I heard Reba McEntire singing on the radio. I can't remember the title. Right now all I know is I keyed in on one verse which is so true. "If dreams give you power/Then I'm strong enough . . ./and never give up...Obviously, my dream is to be able to walk, but obviously, well, you know. Enough of that . . .

What I'm getting at, what I'm attempting to say here, is that I was a normal, for the most part, kid, teenager, teenage-girl which has added-life-drama on its own, in so many ways. I had the same ebbs and flows, dreams and aspirations, as any other girl my age, except for the added challenges that come with being disabled and in a wheelchair with less than cooperative extremities.

This brings to mind an unfulfilled dream or aspiration I once had. Let me preface that statement with the fact that my parents had always prepped me from a very young age for the idea that someday I would leave home and go away to school. I actually remember being terrified at the thought because I was like four or five when the subject first came up—at which time my parents were helping a distant relative, a second cousin or some such person, move into a college dorm room.

Once I warmed up and accepted the idea, even embracing it, we began looking into the specifics of the renowned (or so we heard) disabled student's program at the University of California, Berkeley—supposedly the best in the country. Our understanding of the program, via brochures and attending, shoot . . .what do you call them . . .college recruitment fairs or expos . . .anyway, my parents and I were under the impression that I would be provided with fully accessible accommodations such as bathroom and living quarters, everything, as well as a full time aide at my disposal, like 24/7, for the four years that I would attend Berkeley . . .for a price, of course. It said so right on all the paperwork—the pamphlets, brochures and informational packets that my parents and I requested and that were mailed to us.

To say the least, we were extremely impressed with what was promised in the black and white text and the glossy colored photos of the facilities. If fact, we were so impressed—and I was serious enough with the entire idea of going to a school like Berkeley and becoming a Golden Bear—that my parents set up a conference call with the director of disabled student services to confirm that what we had been sent, what we read and were told was in fact correct and true.

Take a second here and re-read the paragraph just above this one. Do you see all the words of certainty: fact, promised, correct, true. Guess what, none of it was correct, true, promised, fact, or even honest!

Yes, they had a disabled student services program. Yes, they had accessible dorm rooms with accessible bathrooms. And yes, they had aides for the classroom. They may have even had another aide to assist or do personal care duties, or the one aide may have been one in the same. I don't remember the specifics anymore. It has been a while. What I do remember vividly is what was explained to us about the aide situation during that call. I was going to say it went something like this, but it went exactly like this. (Let me remind you that I am a quadriplegic in a wheelchair having absolutely no ability to move my body mass on my own—like not even rolling over in bed.)

The director said, "The first year, everything, all the staff, is covered by the university, so there will be no cost to Jennifer or her family. (That was nice, I thought.) The second year," he said, "is when they would teach Jennifer how to balance a checkbook, hire her own people, her own help and shop for herself." What the FFFFFFF . . .? I thought. Give me a break was my very next thought. Hummm, at this point I was a junior in high school and had been balancing my check book for years at my mother's insistence. Yes, she physically did it, but I told her how and what to write and where. I already had bills to pay and had to be aware of where my money was going and how much I had. I tended to want to spend money that I didn't have before I started taking charge of my own check book. And shopping! Really!!!!!! I don't think I have ever, to this day, bought anything that wasn't off the clearance rack for years! Or at least that is where I always started.

But that wasn't the kicker. The real untruth and the part that scared my parents to death, and to be honest, pissed me off, was the aide reality and misrepresentation. As I look back, I bet it had something to do with trust, responsibility, accountability: that kind of thing. I could be wrong, but I could be right. What am I talking about? It was explained that said- aide would put me to bed at ten p.m., for example, and be back at eight a.m. the following morning to dress, feed, etc.

This was my parents' take on that: YA, THAT ISN'T HAPPENING! Why so dramatic, you might ask. Again, I stress the fact that I am basically dependent on someone else for pretty much all my physical needs, and this is what they immediately envisioned: My aide, I'll say it is a 'her,' probably being twenty-something (as I later learned, the Disabled Students Department of most higher-learning establishments feel the need, believe it more suitable for some reason—probably in an effort to help the disabled student feel more normal—to pair a disabled-student with a peer, hoping it to be the right-choice, the right-fit for all the right- reasons), either has a bad day or a really good day. What happens? What am I talking about? I'm talking about being at the mercy of someone else's mood, someone who is not a family member, someone who's J.O.B. it is to take care of you. Just as an example or a 'what if' kind of situation, let's say on Wednesday night her boyfriend breaks up with her and she is so distraught, and hung over, that she just can't make it to work, to her J.O.B. Thursday morning and doesn't call "a-n-y-o-n-e." Now remember, she got me settled into bed around ten p.m. on Wednesday night, and even though she is in a dorm room next door, I have seen no one since then. Eight a.m. rolls around on Thursday morning and no aide. I need to pee. Need I say more?

Now, understand, that does not even take into consideration that I might get sick during the night or have to pee, which you know happens, with no one there. My mother even went so far as to visualize in horror being put to bed on a Friday night and not having anyone show up until Monday morning with me having no way to phone home. All she could think of was the endangerment, neglect, and mistreatment that would go on without her even knowing. And I can tell you, parents, especially mama bears, can and will think of everything "not good" you could possible think of—and mine did.

Longer story short: I never made it to a campus tour, nor did I become a Golden Bear. I suppose the moral of this story is: start early, because from my experience, at least for me anyway, it takes a while to warm up to a new idea. It takes time and in-depth due-diligence to gather all and I mean <u>ALL</u> the information you need—not what is said or promised, but what is true. And here is a chuckle moment for you, for years I cried because I had to go, and then I cried because I couldn't.

Berkeley now being off the table, I, for the most part, moved onto "Plan B," which had its own set of obstacles and challenges. But before that I fully enjoyed my senior year in high-school.

One of the things that comes to mind was attending my first high-school play, which happened to be *Oklahoma*, with my aide Debbie and her husband, Mark. There was nothing significant about going to the play, other than the fact that it took my English teacher, Mrs. Brodrick, four-years to get me into the theatre to see one of her productions.

Maybe, now that I think about it, going to that play *was* important.

Mrs. Brodrick wasn't one of my favorite teachers early on, but by the time I became a senior, I may have grown up a bit, and she had made it to the top, not the very top, but near the top of my favorites' list.

Initially she had annoyed me by insisting on getting me on stage to perform. I wasn't that kind of performer. I knew my abilities and desires, which definitely did not include drama and still doesn't to this day. But she wanted me to take drama. To do that, I would have had to drop some Ag classes. That was a no-go for me. She got the tiniest bit weird when I said no, because she was a diva in her own-right, and no one had ever dared push-back until the day I did. Eventually we came to some sort of unspoken truce.

In hindsight, I wish I had seen more of her plays. I wish I had not been such a snot. Because of my orneriness, I had missed some great opportunities and awesome shows, but it had been a stick-to-my-guns kind of thing.

I've spoken quite a bit about inclusion in my life, in this book and in other books I have written. There was a plethora of moments, of times, that my schoolmates, peers, friends, included me wholeheartedly, without reservation. But in my senior year of high school there were a few that will stay with me for my lifetime.

One of those moments was being voted FFA Barn Dance Queen. Yep, back to FFA! Granted, the honor was somewhat of a popularity contest. Now that that is said and out of the way, there was actually more to it than the popular vote. There was a combination of components that had to be met to don the coveted FFA Queen belt buckle. First of all, one had to be in good standing. I'm not even sure what that means, but good grades, no prison record . . .that kind of stuff I'm assuming.

Secondly, there was a fund raising element. I opted to raise and raffle off a lamb—cut and wrapped. Luckily, showing their support, all my friends and family helped me sell raffle tickets, which put me way over and above the amount raised by all the other contestants. I remember spending several weekends sitting behind a table loaded with raffle tickets in front of my mom's place of employment. She worked at a restaurant in a tourist town. Such a lucrative location! I mean, people who are hungry seemed to buy anything related to food.

(Okay, I really need to mention something here especially since I am delving into popularity, maybe the pulling of heart strings of people, and y'know the ever-present sympathy aspect of being on four wheels instead of two legs. Do you remember ever hearing the old saying, "Use what your mama gave you"? Well, over the years, I figured that out. In the raffle ticket situation, I mean, who is going to walk by the poor wheelchair-bound girl and not buy a measly $1 ticket. The funny thing is, I was able to share my, what should I call it . . .I'll call it exactly what it is . . .my disability with others. I remember one time going to a Daryle Singletary concert being escorted to the floor of the convention center, right up and personal to the stage, instead of having to sit in the stands. In this particular instance, the small group of friends I was with got to accompany me as well. I'm trying to say that being disabled is always bad, but there are advantages, sometimes. I know it sounds kind of weird, playing the "feel sorry for me card" when I keep talking about normal independence and all, but who would not take advantage of an opportunity if it is presented to them? It is kind of human nature, I think. I was able to, go with me here, have and share my own kind of inclusion, inclusion into my life.)

Anyway, back to the queen thing. A third component was a test, verbal in my case, on FFA history and so forth. It was kind of awesome to be able to basically redo my freshman bombing of the regional greenhand competition . . .and then some. The culmination of all the parts, the fundraising, the written test of FFA knowledge, and yes, even including the popularity vote: I proudly won the buckle.

Another one of those most memorable times of inclusion was, OMG!, Debbie and Nino, don't kill me! My first drink . . .illegal first drink, mind you. I don't know if this qualified as a kids-will-be-kids thing, but we all know we all did it. Let me set scene:

Senior prom. We all went, date or not. First of all, that morning my mom and I were summoned to the school barn by one of the students who was responsible for one of the school's bred sows. The sow was in labor and having problems. Long story short, while I spent the entire time wondering if I'd even make it to prom now, we spent the biggest part of the day babysitting said-pig. The day ended with Mom's arm up the sow's butt, up to her shoulder, pulling out like ten or twelve baby piglets. The number escapes me right now.

Our job done. Pig stink gone, hair and makeup done, and dressed to kill, if I do say so myself, I was ready for Debbie, my aide, my date for the evening. We started the evening with dinner at the local family pizza place, Nino's. While ordering our meals, I noticed a look pass between Debbie and Nino. I really didn't recognize the look at the time, but put two and two together when the glass of wine showed up in front of me. Was I apprehensive? Yes! Was I going to turn it down? No! Debbie's only request was that I not tell anyone on her, even my mom. Nino followed suit making me swear not to tell half the town that was going to be at the prom, kids and chaperones alike. Debbie followed my 'cross my heart and hope to die' promise with "It's not like you're going to drive a car or anything." Looking back, I think they truly wanted me to have the full senior prom experience, booze and all, even 7-up laced white wine.

The last one before I moved on up and out of high school, the last act of inclusion bestowed upon me, was a collaborative collection of thought and action from my entire graduating senior class. Each year as a tradition, whatever senior class is graduating gives the school a gift, passes on a tribute, so to speak. The year I graduated my class opted to build and donate a wheelchair ramp that was to become part of the graduation stage. Why was this an act of inclusion?, you might ask . . .Well, it is a least two-fold. Let me explain.

There had been a girl in a wheelchair before me who graduated. I rode the handicapped bus with her my freshman year, her senior year. She was a very quiet girl, pretty much a loner, and didn't like to rock the boat or even be noticed. I don't think her classmates even really knew her well. When she graduated, she did not make the walk up to and across the stage in celebration of her achievement. She didn't even move from where she had been sitting in her wheelchair during the entire ceremony. Her diploma was unceremoniously walked down to where she was sitting and handed to her.

My graduating class was not having that. It was obviously important to me to participate and "walk" with my class, but it was as important for my class to have me on stage and walk with them. The second part of the two-fold gift and donation to the school was that I may have been the first to use the ramp but there were other disabled—not all wheelchair- bound—but students in need of ambulatory assistance who were coming up behind me. My graduating class took the idea, the bull by the horns, taking the idea of inclusion to a whole other level.

In the same vein, but perhaps on a smaller scale, my graduating class made sure I was able to participate fully in the graduation process and preparation. Silly, maybe, but it meant the world to me. When caps and gowns were delivered I was offered, persuaded even, by the adult/parent graduation committee to take mine home to put on privately prior to my arrival at the school gym where staging was to take place. Again, my classmates were not having it. They put their foot down against all adult . . .what should I call it . . .pressure, perception,

influence concerning the right thing to do for me. The funny thing is there seemed to be two competing definitions of "the right thing to do"—one from parents and one from kids. In a previous book, as well as earlier in this book, I explained that I believe that discrimination and prejudice is a learned behavior due to the influence of adults. That didn't quite happen with or to the kids I had grown up with for the last twelve academic and social years. They knew me; they "learned" me; they loved me . . .Too much? Well they at least liked me; they always included me.

Prior to graduation my parents and I, along with school officials, began to research my options for higher learning. I wasn't going to be attending Berkeley, but I was going to go somewhere. That somewhere was the local junior college, Gavilan, where most of us went before going "away" to school. Hey, most of us weren't dummies. Why pay for room and board while taking general education classes when you can live at home on your parent's dime until you have to declare a major and specialized areas of interest.

My biggest hurdle, although there were more than you could imagine and crazier than you could imagine, was the fact that I would no longer be provided an aide through the San Benito School system. I'd no long have an IEP (Individual Education Plan). Now at the age of eighteen, I was considered an adult and on my own. Lol . . .not really. I was now the County and or State's responsibility, problem, issue . . .pick one. It seems that once I turned eighteen, I was no longer my mother's child to take care of, pay for or whatever else mothers do for their children. She basically had to apply for the same job she had done for eighteen years, a paying job now, mind you, and became my In-Home Support Service Care Provider. Why? Because, I guess it is the law. To this day my niece, who is now eleven-years-old, can't wrap her head around the idea of my mother, her grandmother, getting paid to take care of me, her aunt. "Like you wouldn't take care of her anyway?" was her point-blank response when it was explained to her.

Back to the beginnings of my hurdles, my transition to junior college. We began by setting up a meeting with all those people and departments I had been supported by, not only through high school, but from kindergarten on up, and the new agencies, and governmental support programs, such as the Department of Rehabilitation that I would now be dealing with. I am singling them out for a specific reason, a most vivid memory of a crazy-ass-mother really beginning to understand the inadequate knowledge some of those new employees have. I have to add: this is even after the in-depth meeting we all attended where I recall feeling like a volleyball being tossed back-and-forth, being spoken about and not to, because "they" all thought they had the best answers, suggestions, and whatnot, with my best interest in mind.

So, after my mom secured her position as my "provider," my Department of Rehabilitation case worker (I'll call her Mary) mailed a time-sheet to her listing two-and-a-half hours for paid assistance. Understand that my mother didn't want to go to school with me in the first place. As a side note, she expressed how she hated school when she was a kid and did not relish the idea of going back with me. But, for some reason, that was what was determined was going to happen. I'll get into that topic later. Anyway, confused, my mom called Mary and asked about the discrepancy in what was discussed at the volleyball meeting and what was written on paper. Now realize that I was only hearing half of the conversation and it made no sense at all, but my mom was more than irate. To the best of my knowledge, as she explained after she got off the phone, it went something like this:

> Mom: I just got the paperwork for two and a half hours of time. Jenni will be in school for six hours a day, five days a week during which time she will need an aide.
>
> Mary: That amount is for bathroom and feeding assistance. We don't pay for note takers.

(This is a statement that had been made by Mary about nine hundred and seventy-three thousand times in preparation for college.)

>Mom: I got that! I'm not talking about taking notes. I'm talking about Jenni sitting in class not able to perform any of the tasks needed or asked of her. Please keep in mind that she has had a one-on-one aide all through school.
>
>Mary: We do not provide or pay for note takers.
>
>Mom (now absolutely livid): FOR GOD'S SAKE!!! Would you do me a favor?

(Mom said she had a visual image of Mary doing as she asked, as she answered with a bit of a quiver in her voice.)

>Mary: Okaaaay.
>
>Mom: Sit on your hands, and pretend you are in math class. The teacher says to turn to page nine and ten and do problems fourteen and fifteen.
>
>Mary (quite indigently): Well, I can't do that sitting on my hands!

Mom: No shit!

Mary: Oh, did Jennifer have a one-on-one aide in high school?

Mom: Did I not just say that? Were you not at the same meeting the rest of us were at when all of that was explained and talked about at length?

(She was.)

Mary: Oh, well, yes, I see. I didn't realize. I'll adjust. La de da la de da . . .

A week or so later Mom got a new timesheet with a total of thirty hours of time for the six-hours of classroom time. The twelve-and-a-half hours that was previously given had been taken away. "I'm sorry," Mom sarcastically stated, "you no longer get to pee or eat while you are at school." This was one of those 'pick your battle' kinds of things that we have learned about over time.

Another one of those battles was not long in coming, once again . . .with Mary. A little background might be needed first. Around seventh grade I had the good fortune to hook up with The Library of Congress for The Blind and Dyslexic on tape program. It is a free service, FYI. They not only have literature and for pleasure reading, but they also had textbooks. The reason I enlisted this service was because of a couple of reasons. First of all, I tried using something called a page turner which, unless the book was a hundred years old with broke down binding, didn't work. To tell the truth, some adaptive equipment just doesn't work. It is always a try and see game.

Secondly, I spent way more time waiting for my mother to come turn the pages of my book for me than I did reading. It generally averaged five- minutes of wait-time between probably a three-minute-page-read before she reappeared to turn said-page. This of course was preceded by, "Mom, I'm ready." And, "I'll be there in a second." It was a loooong damn second . . .

So, in preparation for my college classes, as I had done for every year since seventh-grade, I called books on tape and got all of my class text books on tape delivered several weeks before school started. A couple of weeks later, as instructed, I submitted a list of needed books along with a purchase request. This was <u>absolutely</u> one of Depart. Of Rehab. Services. In comes a call from Mary. She asked that we come to the office. We, of course, thought it was to pick up a check for books. Wrong! Somehow she had gotten wind that I had gotten my books on tape and, therefore, had determined that I didn't need the ones I had asked the Depart. Of Rehab. to purchase for me.

OH, ho, ho, ho!!! Once again, mama bear had some 'splaining to do. It boiled down to the fact that I couldn't follow-along in class on tapes. My mother also enlightened Mary to the fact that what we do for ourselves on our own behalf has nothing to do with what her agency is required to do for their clients. And besides, my mother stated, just to prove a point, "How do you know that I didn't get the books for myself?" which, of course, Mary had no answer for.

Sharing these trials and tribulations you might find funny and maybe even helpful. They are sort of meant to be both helpful and funny. But what I really want to do is share the idea of advocacy. Have one, an advocate. Be your own advocate. Fight for it, advocacy. I'm not talking about being a prima donna about things. I'm not talking about being and or acting privileged as in I-deserve-all-this-shit-because-I'm-disabled. There are those kinds of people in every walk of life, disabled or not: the ones who believe they deserve everything they want because it is out there and available, those that feel they are entitled. I'm not saying that I won't try all and everything presented to me to help improve my world. I'm saying if some piece of equipment, for example, doesn't work for me, there is no need to have and to hold onto it, hog it, and in so-doing deprive someone else who may benefit greatly from that piece of equipment, just to say I have it. And believe me, it feels so much "righter" to not take what I don't really need and leave it for someone else who needs it to help them fly.

I'm pretty sure my attitude towards "only taking what I need and leaving the rest" comes from my parents. A perfect example, to this very day, is my mother's philosophy on handicapped parking. As long as I can remember, and I'm sure before that, my mother has always driven the designated vehicles that transport me, with disabled license plates on them. This, of course, gives her the right to park in any "blue parking space" reserved for disabled folk. We also had a placard that always goes with me should I be in some other vehicle. My point here is that my mother never uses, in fact refuses to use said parking space unless I'm with her. There is nothing that irritates us more than confronting a person who undeservingly has parked in that spot who replies with "I was just going to be there for a second," to which my mother never fails to answer with "And it looks like someone needed that spot in that second, doesn't it?"

Then, not once, but twice, my dad had knee surgery and was either using a walker, crutches, or a cane but was still driving . . .on occasion, at first, and never once used the placard. I offered it to him because I considered him "disabled" at the time, lol. "Not mine to use" was his reply.

Speaking of cars and drivers and whatnot just reminded me of the bus driver guy! OMG! I haven't thought about him in twenty plus years. Way funny story here as well as an advocacy thing . . .sort of in reverse.

So back to transitioning from high school to college. My mom, not having yet accepted her fate as becoming my college aide, the area of transportation to and from the college campus was addressed . . .for about a nano-second! Not that my mother was keen on the idea from the get go, but the plan was for me to take public transit; the dial a ride is what we called it back then. Anyway, the bus shows up in front of our house one day for a trial-run. Y'know, how to load me and the wheelchair. How to tie down and secure the wheelchair. All the same stuff we did every time I got a new school bus driver. When the driver clumsily tried to make his way through the unopened accordion doors, I watched as my mom's eyes got as big as plates. I kinda knew something was up.

This guy, the driver, who my mom told me later looked like Harpo Marx, hair and all, had been a bartender for like one shift where my mom was a waitress. After she sent him on his way without letting him get anywhere close to me—let along try and load me onto the bus—and without explanation, she disclosed her reason for doing-so. It turns out that, during his one shift, Mom watched as the guy got stressed, started walking feverishly around in circles, pulling his curlier than curly Harpo Marx hair (okay, sorry, that is mean, but it helps the visual she was selling), and ranting and mumbling something to himself, totally overwhelmed.

Mom also expressed that she could have understood, had it not been two o'clock in the afternoon, the absolutely slowest time of the day . . .like maybe four customers in the whole restaurant. My mother not only declined his services, she said "Hell, NO!" .

Besides the unstable nature of the bus driver, my mom also shared her other concerns with sending me to school on my own. There was a list of them: How do I know she gets there? What happens if no one meets her? It's not like she can call me and tell me she is stranded. What happens if she doesn't make it home? Where do I start looking? And a million more. Major Reality Check! Not all things are awesome!

Basically, mine and my mother's next four years were set for us, due to that one experience: the service that we turned down, which led us to Mary and fighting for the services we did need and want. Mom said it had something to do with "my best interest." Interestingly enough, Mom's first paycheck included compensation for mileage—probably from the transportation fund I was not going to be using. I guess Mary didn't want to tangle with my mother again.

Talk about time warp! This was my thought about going to preschool:

Probably the biggest unknown and frightful thing about preschool happened on the very first day. I wasn't aware of it before-hand, but my mom wasn't spending the day there with me. Well, she wasn't intending to spend the day there with me. I, of course, wasn't too cool with that and had my own rendition of how that first (and every other day) was going to go down. And that "is" what did happen that first day and for some time after. Although, towards the end of the second week I did notice she was more often than not in the teacher's office, outside, or in the kitchen helping prepare snacks or lunch. In other words, away from me. I had to be taught and learn about separation and that I'd be okay.

  This was not how I expected or felt on my first day of junior college. Away from me was what I expected and kinda, sorta wanted. A few weeks into preschool I was left on my own, so to speak. I was beginning to make the move, as any child, from complete parental involvement to close to having next to no parental involvement by high school, at least for me, while at school and socially, anyway. I probably still had more parental involvement than most high-school kids—although I am finding it rather funny that my parents are now learning more about my high-school "going-ons," twenty-some-odd-years later, through this book, than they did back then. Now, I was moving back to massive parental involvement. I was, what I felt, moving backwards, or at least getting my wings clipped. And to tell you the truth, it was the first thing we had to work through, something that we would deal with for the rest of my educational career.

  It wasn't something we had thought about or even considered would be an issue. What am I talking about? I'm talking about a newly found fine line of distinction between my mother and my new complicated relationship that showed itself and had to be dealt with on a minute-by-minute basis. I don't mean to be cryptic here, but you have to understand that my mother was/is my mother who, I guess I should say, alongside my father, ruled the roost at home. They made the rules, decisions, choices; they were the boss of me, so to speak. Here at school, that was the rub: she was not the boss of me! In fact, since she was employed by the Department of Rehabilitation as my aide, more specifically, employed by me, I was the boss of her, at school anyway. But that wasn't altogether true, either. There were times that she inserted her parental opinion or influences when she thought I needed it . . .like using my time wisely when I had free time between classes. I 'may' have wanted to socialize while she thought I should be studying or preparing for my next class. In other words, who is the boss? Who tells whom what to do and when? Are we friends or mother and daughter? And that was it. We, my mother and I, had to learn that we were each of those things at different times, even within a brief span of time.

One of my mom's most telling stories about our 'me-her' scholastic relationship, one that kind of carries over into life in general, is classwork and tests. In earlier years my grandmother had giving my mother crap about not fixing an incorrect answer on a math homework assignment—to which my mother replied, "If it is wrong, it is wrong, and she will figure it out when we go back and do the recheck." Logical, right? A good parental response.

Fast forward fifteen or so years. I vividly remember taking my first test in college. As a disabled student I was allowed extra time and often took exams out of the classroom, usually in the library where I could verbally respond to the questions. As my aide, my mother was also my scribe, and I dictated my answers to her for her to write in the infamous Blue Book or Scan-Tron. The first test was a Scan-Tron. As I gave my mother my answers to questions she either colored in the appropriate letter or paused and asked, "Are you sure?," sort of re-enacting my grandmother's 'fix it' thought process.

I remember staring stupidly at her, thinking, "Oh crap! She is my mother. How am I going to buck her 'mother authority,' without pissing her off and tell her to stop and leave it alone? If it is wrong, then it is wrong, and it is on me." I actually gathered my courage and said just those words to her, and then she had the most startled stupid look on her face. It never happened again. I'm thinking she recalled her conversation of my math homework with her mother and understood. Some years later her recollection about testing was rather humorous. She likes to share that ninety-nine percent of the time what she thought was the right answers were, in fact, wrong, and mine were right on.

I've mentioned math a couple of times here but not my distain for it. We all know that fulfilling general education requirements includes a few math elements. Yuck! One of the two math classes I opted for was statistics—an odd choice for someone who hates math, I agree. But I somehow realized the statistics calculator did most of the work for me because it had all the appropriate formulas programmed into it, and I duly appreciated that fact: that is, until the chapter on probabilities came around. This brought up an unforeseen problem. I had never handled a deck of playing cards, due to my less than minimal fine or gross motor dexterity. Why was that a problem? Well, because, I had no clue that there were fifty-two cards in a deck—an extremely important piece of 'prior knowledge' to own when discussing—you got it—probabilities.

What do playing cards have to do with probabilities? For Mr. Bates, the instructor, everything . . .his go-to probability example was always a deck of fifty-two cards. For those of you who are mathematically-challenged, as I am, let me explain. One of the first scenarios Mr. Bates (yes, that was really his name) presented to the class was this: If you pull a king out of a deck and then return it to the deck, what is the probability that you would pull a king out of the deck again? I have no idea what the answer is anymore, but in order to figure it out, one needs to know what you start with, which in this case is fifty-two.

So, as I sat in class listening to the question above, I realized I didn't possess a key bit of information. That becoming evident, I quietly attempted to get my mom/aide's attention to ask her how many friggin' cards are in a deck of cards. She was feverishly taking notes as she always did in class for me and kept waving her hand and "shushing" me. Finally, she looked up and said, "What?"

"How many cards are in a deck of cards?" I frantically but simply asked.

She stared at me blankly and then started to laugh. "Yeah, that might be helpful information to have."

That night after class my mom got out a deck of cards and laid them on the kitchen table, first in groups of the four suits and explaining that to me, and then each suit in sequence of ace to king. As she shared the values of the different cards, it reminded me of the game Yahtzee, and I said so. "By God, she had it all the time!" my mom joked.

Along with sharing my hatred for math, I primarily wanted to share the idea that tactually-based tasks (like when kids use their fingers to count with) were and are a challenge for me. But as a rule, with experimentation and trial and error, my parents most always figured out a way for me to fuse the senses, the abilities that I did and do have in order to complete any given task: like when I was in grade-school and learned that Italy and Greece were best represented and remembered as the boot and below and that nine and any number is one less than the number you're adding the nine to—$9+8=17$.

I also have to mention that my unique way of thinking or learning things was also beneficial to classmates, even at the college level. I remember one specific evening showing up for class early, as I did frequently, because in my mother's eyes, "If you aren't early, you are late." I never did get it, but whatever . . .Anyway, there had been a take home test which no one was able to complete. Knowing I had a better handle on the principles and theories than most of them, (an idea that was super shocking to me, BTW) a large group bombarded me with questions on how I solved the problem on the test. I spent the time we had, not giving them the answers, but explaining how I got the answers I did. I don't think Mr. Bates really ever knew or understood why or how his students all of a sudden had a better grasp on statistics. I think they just began to learn differently.

This brings me to Gavilan's Disabled Students Services and its tutoring department—a wonderful group of people who were uniquely placed in a room, a space, down a short hall off the library! (This is important, and I'll expand on it in a minute.) Just as my parents had always done, they also helped me to learn with the abilities I had and how to navigate around those that I did not have. It is very difficult to describe to someone who is not disabled having to learn in a non-traditional fashion. All children learn to count on their fingers, unless your fingers don't work. Then what do you do? You have someone lay crayons out on a table or desk for you to count. And these people had been doing exactly that for years for many of the college's disabled students: tucked away, knowing their clientele, so to speak. (This is as opposed to the school's even being aware of the needs or requirements of their disabled students.)

I'm not saying the junior college didn't provide what I needed or make adaptions to classrooms, desks, testing accommodations, and such, because they did. However, something that we found totally comical, and quite honestly we could never understand, was why there was an automatic door opener to the library itself but not one on the door to the entryway of the Disabled Students Services tutoring center where more than myself were in wheelchairs, walkers, or other adaptive mobility aids. I was not the first to bring up the issue. It seemed to be a long-standing joke among the Disabled Services Department workers and students . . .like forever. We used to laugh at the fact that we could get into the library but not, as disabled students, into the Disabled Students Department. Go figure . . .it is kind of like the whole "sit on your hands" thing my mother made the Department of Rehabilitation woman do in order to get her to understand what was needed. It was never addressed or "fixed" the four years I attended the school. It could still be that way. I don't know. It might very well have been one of those "pick your battle" situations for the Department.

  All this talk of Gavilan College brings back lots of memories. One in particular makes me chuckle every time I think about it and how absolutely stupid we were. My mother drove a full-size van which had a hydraulic side-lift for my wheelchair. As I mentioned before, I was not the only student in a wheelchair. One of those fellow students was Monica, a good friend of mine. One day she needed to do more than go home. She needed to go to the bank. Have I mentioned yet that I am blonde? Well, I had a really blonde-moment and told Monica, since we were leaving right then anyway, we could give her a ride to the bank and home. And although my mother is not blonde, she, in her "we'll give it a shot" modus operandi agreed to at least attempt the endeavor. We really didn't even know if we could get two wheelchairs in the van. Of course, it was probably totally against the law and any rational thinking person's common sense, but with some advanced

Tetris-playing we got both wheelchairs in the van, and off we went, totally proud of our accomplishment. After the fact, realizing the bone-headed nature of our accomplishment—we never did it again—my mother and I vowed never to tell a soul . . .until now, of course.

Another one of those 'give it a shot' instances was when I was referred to the computer lab to possibly assist me in my painting. Wait have I mentioned that I paint with my less than operable hands? Yes, I do! My mom used to call it finger painting, but it is actually something called Abstract Expressionism. Who would have thought what I did had a name? Yep, this little diva paints like the infamous Jackson Pollock.

Back to the story. I tried computer painting, and it wasn't the same thing as me pushing and pulling paint, closing and opening my hands, on paint boards or canvas. Even though a computer is a computer and 'supposedly' non-thinking, it totally interfered with my process: my movement, my feelings, my emotions, my color choices. It was kind of cool to try, but it didn't work for me.

Another computer fail was the voice-activated assistive-computer program which was also suggested by the computer-lab people and supported by a trip to Stanford for an evaluation. Like the page turner that didn't perform well for me, all conditions need to be optimum for equipment to have any chance in hell of working. We tried Dragon Speaks first, for example. This consisted of "teaching" the computer not only my voice but also my speech patterns. Remember me describing my speech as CP-babblelistics? The computer was not at all well versed in CP-

Even Broken-Winged Divas Can Fly

babbleistics and never worked for me. When I laughed it wrote—ten, ten, ten, ten, ten, ten, ten, which made me laugh even more and caused the computer to continue to write the number ten.

The Stanford computer specialist team tried other fancy assistive devices and elaborate apparatuses, and all very expensive, pretty much to no avail. I even remember having a Baliwood kind of dot placed on my forehead to aim at an on screen keyboard. Again, laughing, I couldn't keep my head still enough for it to work. The upside to that all day trip to Stanford was getting dinner at a restaurant of my choice out of the deal on the way home.

After all that time and advanced technology, and there was more than that one trip and equipment testing, to this day I use the "mickey-moused" together skateboards wrist-guard with a pencil taped, eraser side down, between my thumb and pointer finger—the one my mother and occupational therapist came up with many moons ago, like when I was in grade school. Sometimes some of the simplest, the least technological, things are the best. This is opposed to just having someone else be my scribe: at this point in my life, the fastest and most productive mode of operation because I have way more to say that I did in grade school.

When my time at Gavilan Junior College was coming to an end, so was my dad's time of punching the time-clock. He was on the road to retirement. You'd think the usual course of events would have me moving away, away from home and parents, to attend a four-year college somewhere. That is in fact what both my sister and brother did. And moving I was but not alone. Long story here. Not even going to try and make it short!

Let me set the stage. At this point in time I had lived in the same house for seventeen years and in the same town for twenty-plus years. If you are reading this book because you have a disabled, maybe wheelchair-bound child or person living with you, you may know where I am going here. Living in that same house, one that had over the years been adapted to my needs (bathroom and such: changes and adaptions I was accustomed to and that made life easier for me), I knew where to turn wide, where to ask for help, what rugs I could turn on without bunching them up (I hate area rugs, BTW), how far I could venture out onto the patio without falling off the edge: all that stuff most people don't have to think about. Familiarity: I was losing all that I was familiar with and knew how to navigate.

On the flip side the house my parents bought was a new build, and they were able to customize the house to accommodate my needs before we even moved in. I remember meeting our new neighbors and them commenting that they had peeked at the house as it was being built and that we sure had a lot of tile in the house. After meeting me, they now understood why.

Setting aside all of the customizing of the new house, as cool as it was, I still had to learn a new floor plan and how to navigate new corners, new hallways, new counters, and where I could and couldn't go or go by myself. And let me tell you, I had five long months to practice in a temporary, what should I call it, holding-pattern house. Again, let me explain. (Remember, not a short story!) We put our house up for sale thinking it would take several months to sell, and if need be, we could live in a long-term hotel or something of that nature for a couple of weeks or so. Not the way it happened! Ten days after listing it was sold, and we had thirty days to move to a house that was not yet finished! Panic to say the least . . .three people, three dogs, and a house full of shit with no place to put any of it.

Aunt Karen and Uncle Pete to the rescue! They happened to have a rental house in the next little town over that they were revamping to sell. It was empty at the time, and they offered it to us for the five-month duration. It was a little bitty shotgun house, you know, the kind where you walk into the living room from the front door and from there straight into the kitchen. It had two bedrooms and one bathroom. My brother was still living with us at the time and also attending Gavilan College: so four people, three dogs with a minimal amount of belongings and furniture. I imagine you are thinking that four people and two bedrooms don't add up, and you are right. My parents got one bedroom, and my brother got the second bedroom. Where did that leave me? In the non-descript four-foot space between the living room and the kitchen. No walls. Just space. Privacy? What was that? Unfair you think? Not really, because the hallway to the bedrooms was so narrow that I couldn't make the turn into either one with or without help. To this day my mom laughs when she shares the bedroom story, one of the stories she loves telling about our stay in what we called the San Juan house.

Thinking back on that time, I recall that we did a whole lot of "make it work," I don't know, shenanigans, maneuvering—I can't even call them adaptions—and goofiness. We made do with what we had, and not just for me but pretty much for all four of us living there. The bedroom story? It was about me sitting in the living room and getting pissed off about something, who knows what, and dramatically stating, "I'm going to my room!" And then, in a less than theatrical movement, backed up two feet and flipped around so my back was to the living room and the people in it. My anger lasted for only a split second because I heard my mother bust up laughing. Hearing her laughter made me realize just how what I was doing was silly and flat-out hysterically funny. It had lost the dramatic effect I had hoped for, because, well, because, well, just picture it . . .a temper tantrum only works if you have somewhere to go and can stomp off doing so.

So I guess there really wasn't much navigating in the straight line I had to travel, except for the makeshift ramp to get into the house because of the steps to the porch, and to and in the bathroom—which of course, I could never do by myself. And let me tell you about the bathroom . . .

First and most obvious, four people, one bathroom with one toilet and all of us needing to be up and out of the door in the morning for various reasons: work, school, and so forth. We had to make that work for sure, so yes, we had to set up a schedule as to who got the bathroom when, which turned out wasn't a problem. The problem was 'how long' the 'when' was. I know, totally confusing, right?

Maybe some of you can relate . . .I don't know if it is a disabled thing, a girl thing. I know it can be an old people thing. Can it be a guy thing? I don't know. And this may be a TMI thing, but this is one of those things, one of those questions that I have been asked a bazillion times: bath-rooming and how it is done.

Over the years I have had a variety of toilet/bath chairs and generally had (still do) more than one, usually stashed in a closet somewhere, all for the purpose of ICE (in case of emergency). In fact, I even have one that lives at my sister's house, and has for years, because we are there so often.

Living in that little shot-gun house and using multiple toilet/bathroom chairs was not really an ICE situation but more or a logistical one. Remember I said that I couldn't get into the bathroom by myself. In actuality, my wheelchair didn't fit in the bathroom at all. So where did that leave me? It left my wheelchair in the hall with my mother lifting and carrying me to the toilet/bath chair either in the bathtub or over the toilet itself. Here is the logistical part, why I used two potty/shower chairs. If I were going to use the toilet prior to taking a shower I had to be transferred from wheelchair to toilet and, instead of back to the wheelchair so the one potty seat could be moved from the toilet to the shower (which was a tub/shower combo that created its own set of issues), before I was moved, once again from my wheelchair to the seat, one seat lived on the toilet and one lived in the shower. To be honest, and I may be going way TMI here—but it's all about being honest, right? I was not above skipping the toilet (as long as I only had to pee) and going straight to the shower and . . .do I really need to spell it out? As convoluted and complicated as this paragraph is, so was the actual act of getting me up and ready for the day while living in a temporary home.

Wait, now that I think back, maybe that's a lie. My parents were particularly careful with the maneuvering of my wheelchair so as not to mess up walls and door jams because we were renting the house. I do remember one evening my aunt was "hanging out" with me while my parents were off doing something-or-other, and I needed to pee. As my aunt and I headed to the bathroom I told her that I didn't fit and explained that we had been being very careful not to nick or chunk out walls and doorways. She responded with, "Thank you for that, but I own the house, and the closer I get you to the toilet the easier it is for me." After a chink here and there, me, my wheelchair and my aunt were snuggly in the smallest room in the house . . .together. "See, we fit!" was all she said with a smug smile on her face. I also may recall that it was a little more difficult getting out. I also recall telling her that SHE was telling my parents how the doorway got messed up.

Somehow I seemed to have gotten of topic: the one bathroom with four people and all of us needing to be up and out of the door at basically the same time topic. The problem of 'how long' the 'when' was, was a real issue for me. Let me explain, first by asking a question. How do preform under pressure? Me—and I'm going to blame it all on the cerebral palsy, I suck! I'm also going to guess again that you are reading this book because you have some knowledge of cerebral palsy or some other disability and understand or want to understand the physical, muscular, mental weirdnesses—those that are bestowed upon our bodies, and how they may connect in and to our lives in general, and how they interact, whether we want them to or not.

A lot of confusing information, I know. Thus, the one bathroom, four people scenario. It is the perfect example. Stay with me here.

It is my allotted time in the bathroom. I am basically relaxed since I just got out of bed, but I do have a niggling in my brain that my time is limited which causes just a pinprick of stress to tickle at the back of my neck. Now, if you know anything about CP, you know that there is always a muscle tension issue to deal with. Some are tight and stiff; some are floppy, and some are spastic, and some are combination of some or all of the above, all to varying degrees. I am lucky enough to have a combination of muscle tension issues: stiff, tight, and spastic.

So, although I started out pretty relaxed, the circus in my head begins to take hold, and I find myself tensing up thinking about how I have to hurry up, get going . . .literally, shower, and be ready to pass the room onto my brother.

I'm sure you have heard the old saying that everything in life is a process, and I have to tell you that I totally try and prepare and embrace that idea. I'm talking about things like intentionally not drinking a lot of water so I don't have to pee so much, which of course creates other problems. I'm sure you know what I mean: an act that needs absolute relaxation to complete. Except . . .for me, once the "process" has been interrupted, it just plain stops. Once I've psyched myself out about needing to hurry, everything tenses up and shuts down. I'm talking about every muscle I own, especially my brain (if that is considered a muscle I've already expressed my distain for math, and science is right up there with it as represented by my one and only D in high school). Okay, I know it isn't really a muscle but gray and white matter, an organ, but it does contain muscle tissue that . . .does something-or-other. You thought I was going to get all scientific there and disprove my earlier statement about not liking science, didn't you? Fooled you! Only because cerebral palsy is a condition brought on by a lack of oxygen to the brain, for any number of reasons, do I have some sort of working knowledge of the brain, my brain.

Back to sharing a bathroom on a time schedule and knowing that someone was waiting for their turn always brought me to the point of tension, stress, freaking out, and major muscle shutdown. That means I have to start the whole relaxation process over again. What I am trying to share is that if I know that I am impeding someone's needs or in someone's way because I'm not "moving" fast enough—be it on the toilet or driving my wheelchair down an isle in the grocery store—I get stressed out, freeze up, and can't move at all. I guess the bottom line is, don't be stopping me in the middle 'cause you need to take a quick pee because the whole process, my whole process, has to start over. If I know you need to go and I am preventing you from going, I can't.

Enough potty talk. Let's talk about my twenty-first birthday. First of all, as you may have guessed, my parents were and have always been open-minded about most everything. This also included things like . . .oh, I don't know . . .drinking? Yes, it was something my siblings and I were allowed to do at home, in moderation, on rare occasions, under my parents supervision, with no option of leaving home under any circumstances. On my twenty-first birthday, however, I was allowed, for the first time, to drink (wink, wink . . .remember Nino's?) in public and do so legally.

Because my mom worked at a local Mexican restaurant with a full bar, and because her boss had known my twenty-first birthday was happening, he asked her to bring me to the restaurant for a birthday dinner. He said he had "something" special planned for me but not to tell me, not that she knew what was going to take place. I opted to invite my two longest time aides, Becky and Debbie, to help me celebrate my big milestone, my coming of age, I guess you call it, because God knows, they had been through so many others with me.

When we arrived at the restaurant the whole place seemed to know who we were and why we were there. It was only a little unnerving because I was used to garnering attention because of the oddity of the wheelchair in which I traveled. Being an oddity was not odd for me at all and still isn't.

The oddity that night was feeling that unsettling "something-is-up vibe" in the room. And it wasn't long before I figured out what it was that was up.

A SHOT! A shot was up! A tequila shot was up! Now, for most people, there is a whole ritual that takes place when "doing a shot of tequila," right? There is salt, lime, and a shot-glass full of tequila, which there are varying degrees of quality of. Salt goes on the hand to be licked, shot drunk down, then lime sucked, and then, as I have over the years observed, a whole body-shake or -shiver occurs.

Carlos, my mother's boss, had spent some real time thinking and figuring out how I could best get the full experience of my first tequila shot. He had known me for years and knew my physical limitations, including the inability to feed myself. I remember a song that goes "Put the lime in the coconut, and drink it on down," and that is pretty much what Carlos did or what he did reminded me of. He put the lime in the tequila in a salt-rimmed shot-glass, and I drank it on down to the dismay of Becky, Debbie, and half of the restaurant. As my mom tells the story, she had a plan to nip in the bud any future desire I might have to drink. She held the glass up to my lips and proceeded to say, "If you are going to do this, you are going to do it all the way. Are you ready to shoot it?" I answered in the affirmative, and the next moment I felt the glass press against my lips and tip the "beverage" into my mouth. The next thing I heard was people shouting at my mom to

"Stop! Stop!" (and something like "You're going to choke or drown her," or words to that effect). Her response to them was the same as what she said to me before I shot the shot: "If she's going to do this, she's going to do it all the way!"

The only problem with my mother's plan was . . .I liked it. To this day, my mom shares how her expected outcome didn't play out like she thought. She thought by making me shoot the tequila that it would burn on the way down and cause me to cough, spit, and sputter, and vow never to drink again. She says that, to her surprise, I didn't cough, spit, or sputter but produced a gigantic Cheshire cat smile across my face followed by a little giggle. I remember telling her, "That was nice and warm. I liked it. May I have another?" It was at that point my mother knew that her plan had been an epic fail.

And that was the last birthday celebration I would have in my home-town, as later that year we, my mother and father and I, moved to a little town called Hughson, not to be confused with Houston which is what most people thought I was saying. By that time, my father had retired, and I was ready to move on up to a four-year university and pursue my BA and eventually, it turned out, my Master's Degree. I'm sensing you scratching your head about there being a university in a little town, but Hughson is just a stone's throw, like seven miles, from Turlock, in Stanislaus County, home of CSU,

Stanislaus, a.k.a. Turkey Tech. Again, I bet you are wondering why that location. What made that area so attractive to us. Well, there were a couple of reasons. Actually there were three things that needed to come together all in one location. In Hughson housing was still affordable; there was a four-year university, and that was about as far north as we could go and still have Kaiser Insurance. Of course we could have moved to one of the bigger towns in the area, but my parents tend to like smaller communities.

To back up a bit, insurance is kind of a big deal in today's society for everybody, but especially for those who have chronic conditions or issues, such as being disabled. I was born into the Kaiser insurance company or program, or whatever you want to call it, and since I was born into that specific insurance system, they, I want to say "by law," could not drop my coverage. On the other had if we were to move and change to a different insurance company or plan, the new company could put something called "riders" on me or my coverage which either is much more costly or disqualifies a person with pre-existing conditions, i.e. cerebral palsy, in my case. Kaiser was a familiar entity for my family because it was the insurance my dad had even before there was a "my mom." And I say "was" because things do change. I'll come back to that later. So if you picked up this book for informational purposes . . .keep that in mind.

I'm sure you have heard the saying, *It's a small world.* Well, not too long after we moved to Hughson, my mom and I went to the grocery store in order to sort of scope-out the small shopping center which the grocery store was part of. Remember my first drink at Nino's Pizzeria in Hollister? Lo and behold! as we walked down the sidewalk, there sat Nino on a bench in front of the store! In Turlock, mind you! Not expecting to see him and not realizing it "was" him, we walked right past Nino. It wasn't until he called out my name that we turned, wondering who the heck knew me in this new town. "Oh, My God! NINO?!" were the first words out of my mouth. Turns out, he had sold the restaurant a year or two before (which I knew), retired, and moved to Turlock to be near his grandkids. And bless his damn heart, he spilled the beans. What I mean is . . .my mom never knew about my illegal glass of wine on prom-night three years earlier. In our travels down memory lane, Nino being Nino, he had to mention how he and Debbie had planned the whole thing out, how they planned to help me have the Whole—Entire—Prom—Experience   ...booze and all! Although I had never spoken of the wine up until that point, and my mom had no clue it had happened, she suddenly recalled my expressed dire-need to brush my teeth before going to bed that night. "Well," she laughed out loud, "it all makes perfect sense now."

A little paranoid, I blurted out, "Nino told me not to tell!"

All Nino could do then was laugh and say, "I never said *I* wouldn't tell anyone. I just made sure *you* didn't."

Talk about a blast from the past. It was truly a wonderful way to start a new chapter in my life, in a new town, at a new school, getting a strength, a boost, I suppose, from an old friend, someone who knew where I came from, who had seen what I had done and already knew what I could do.

You have to agree that moving out of a town you grew up in, a small town you grew up in, where you knew just about everyone, can be hard, traumatic, even. I wasn't the only disabled person in my home-town of Hollister or school, for that matter, but I was the only one in a wheelchair for a long while, which in the beginning made me an oddity. But I was also that odd-ball who wanted to . . .and did . . .take part in everything. If you have read *Little Diva On Wheels*, you may remember me talking about the idea of inclusion and being accepted as part of the whole and not being considered "the other." The move, for me, to Hughson and Stan State, put me back in that odd-ball position. I was once again "the other."

The funny thing is I lived in my hometown for twenty-one years. So being the odd-one-out wasn't a cut-and-dried idea or concept I actually understood or remembered. From the beginning of time, it was more of a gradual integration kind of thing. It was never a 'She can't do this' kind of thing but always a 'How can we make this work?' kind of a thing. That all kind of changed with my association with CSU Stanislaus: not necessarily my first association, like with registration and orientation, although there was a bit of a glitch as to which classes I was instructed to enroll in by those upper-classmen mentors who were assigned the task of guiding and influencing us newbies to develop the appropriate class schedules for ourselves. Hint: obviously, being in a wheelchair is associated with intelligence, right?

My very first on campus face-to-face powwow was with the Disabled Students' Services Department, whom my parents had previously talked to on the phone. Oh, and this building had a door that electronically opened with a push of a button. I later found that the whole campus was mostly ADA compliant, which was something I wasn't used to. It was really kind of weird but in a good way. I wasn't the odd-ball; I wasn't in

Kansas anymore; us handicapped folks were all part of the whole.

Anyway, that department's main goal, objective, and purpose was to support all disabled students attending CSU Stanislaus. Their first objective for me was to take the WPST (Writing Proficiency Standard Test) that is required of all new entering students. My mom and I thought, cool, we can do that, and vocalized that to Chessie, the coordinator of the WPST. And Chessie, who had been working with and supporting disabled students for a bazillion years, picked-up on the "we" portion of my mother's statement.

"Not we," she said, "but she."

Of course, my mom was a little taken-aback to say the least . . .okay, being the mama bear she tends to be, she was pissed. Pausing for a split second to collect her composure, my mother simply said, "What?"

I have to say, Chessie was the BOMB! She very calmly explained to my mom that all students must prove their own "proficiency" without possible injected thoughts or ideas from outside sources or influences. Then, without skipping a beat or giving my mom an opening to object, Chessie continued to explain that a peer, a student, would proctor the test using a computer, therefore, enabling Jennifer to see that what she was saying was in fact, being written by said proctor. I'm guessing Chessie had made that speech a few times before. Still my mom was somewhat skeptical and voiced her concerns. I knew the biggest concern my mom had was the proctor's ability to understand me.

"So, what happens if the proctor doesn't understand her and Jen has to take the test over again?" my mom blurted out in protest. (The WPST is not a free test to take. It was only $25 each time you took it, so not really a big deal unless you had to take it five or six times, the number of times the test could be taken.) "Who's going to pay for it again?"

"Trust me," Chessie assured my mom. "It's going to be fine."

Long story short, it was fine. I passed with flying colors, a score of 8 on my very first attempt, something I later learned was almost unheard of, on the first try, anyway. And Chessie, well she made my mother a believer. And my proctor, Kristen, well she became my first new friend at CSU Stanislaus and shopping buddy. She obviously understood me just fine.

I know you are waiting for the odd-one-out story that I made reference to a couple of pages ago, but I also wanted to share the fact that not all agencies and people working at those agencies are clueless like Mary, from the Department of Rehabilitation, whom my mom blasted on the phone about how book pages were going to get turned in my math class. Also, I'd like to add that . . .maybe-sometimes, Mother doesn't always know best. Wink, wink . . .

And now here I am—or here we are—my mother/aide and I, sitting in my first class of the semester at my new school. WPST done. Registration done. Orientation done. We, as usual, strategically selected an edge-row desk, one that my mother would sit in, in the front of the room, not because I'm a kiss-up that way, but because it gave me the best opportunity to see and hear. In my OCD-ish manner, I had arrived to class more than several minutes early so I could scope-out my best sitting arrangement. (No, I don't really have OCD but do tend to be obsessive about some things . . .and totally type-A.) As the rest of the students began arriving and choosing seats, I began to notice a distinct difference between the students/friends I went to high-school and junior-college with and what was going on now. Instead of people in the class picking seats to be near friends, me included, each and every one of them saw me, stared, and plopped down in a desk as far away from me as they could possibly get . . .until, of course, there were none available but the ones next to me. And those who had to assume residence in those seats did all they could do not to look at me. I'm sure that wasn't the first time I'd received that reaction, but it was definitely the first one I remember, and I have to tell you, it was not only unnerving but also eye-opening for me. (Did I mention I wasn't in Kansas anymore?)

Fast forward several days, after an assignment had been made in that class, which I found out later was "bone-head" English, that I had been wrongly pressed to take—one that I didn't even take in junior-college because I was already far beyond that level of English language and literature—because, y'know, people in wheelchairs are dumb, deaf, and blind. Anyway, I decided to take advantage of the extra time I had and go to the recruitment office and grab one of the recruitment pamphlets for the assignment. The assignment was to read through the pamphlet and discern if it did or did not do a good job of doing what it was supposed to, entice perspective student enrollment. I had just enough time to get to class, okay, you know me by now, more than enough time, and get settled and start reading through the pamphlet and highlight with my favorite pink highlighter the points and or words that could, would, might do the job.

Several minutes later in walked Robert Sledge, the instructor, who immediately zeroed in on the pamphlet I had laying on the desk where my mother was sitting alongside of me. He, nothing short of skipping, came up to my mom and me, grabbed the pamphlet, held it up in the air, and proceeded to exaggeratedly ask me where I had gotten it from and why I had it? The he opened the pamphlet and remarked, "Well, look at that! Look at all the pretty Pink!" At this point I so wanted to crawl into a hole and pull it in after me. I couldn't figure out why the man was making a spectacle out of me. Like, why was he bringing attention to me when I was already the odd-ball-out.

I answered his questions, politely, I must say, even though I wasn't sure he deserved it. "It's for the assignment you assigned having to do with the power of words and how they are used. I got it from the student recruitment office where people go who may have possible interest in attending CSU Stanislaus. I highlighted the different words, phrases, and so forth that sort of emphasizes the good reasons one might like to come to this school."

"But," Rob pressed, "why do you have it now?'

"Because I had the time to go get it and I didn't want to wait until the last minute to get it just in case they ran out of them and so I could start working on the paper."

Again, questioning me in front of the whole class (the definition of embarrassing, I might add) he asked, "But why do you already have it and need to start working on the assignment if it isn't due for a month?"

"Because I don't just write it once!!!!" I sputtered. "Like rough drafts and all, and if I get it to you earlier than the due date I can get your comments and feedback to re-write before I finally hand in the final paper."

It was at that second, when Rob looked around the classroom at the open-mouthed students, smiling and only saying, "Oh, okay, just asking . . ." that I realized he was in fact using me as an example. It was also that very same second, he told me later, that he figured out that I was in no way in the right class.

When that paper was due Rob instructed us to break up into groups of four or five and read each other's papers. We were then to pick what we thought was the best paper and then the best paragraph in that paper. By this time a few people had decided they wouldn't catch whatever it was I had that put me in a wheelchair and were willing to join a group that I was part of, accepting me, so to speak. With that being said, before I was even able to turn around and get myself situated into my group, Rob was standing in front of me looked straight at the paper my mother was holding in her hand and said, "Nope, I'm reading Jennifer's paper because I want to go home in a good mood today." He then grabbed my paper, dramatically turned on his heel and marched back to his desk at the front of the room and smiled slyly. Way to go, Teach . . .make me the object of obnoxiousness and embarrass me again, was all I could think.

Rob didn't even get through my entire paper before he stood up and yelled, "Stop! Everyone! Listen to this . . .(I don't remember exactly what it was that I wrote, but I do remember what he was so excited about.) "Bla, bla, bla bla . . ." (this is the important part) "peppered throughout the pamphlet. Do you hear that? Peppered throughout . . .Jennifer, where or how did you come up with that word . . .peppered?"

I have to tell you, I was pretty dumbfounded. "Aaaaa," I stuttered, "up on top of the page when you are typing in a word document on the computer where it says 'review' there is this thing called a 'thesaurus' where you can type in a word and it will give you a list of other words that mean the same thing that maybe sound better?"

Okay, so I know that last sentence was not a question and the punctuation is more likely than not incorrect, but it was totally a question in my mind as to why I had to explain it to a classroom full of college students, some of whom were full-blown adults, thirty or forty years old, who were re-entering college for one reason or other.

There were many, many more instances when Rob used me as an example for one thing or another. I could go through and list them all, but there would be enough to fill a whole other book. I realized somewhere along the way that he wasn't trying to embarrass me but show his students by example how one should proceed in finding, collecting, and implementing data, information, and so forth into a cohesive, well-written essay or term paper. Since I was way above that level of English academia and knew how to do all of that, I think Rob enjoyed what he called my "quick-witted nature" and the joking relationship we developed early-on. Remember this class was lower than English 101, and that was the only course Rob taught all day long. I don't mean to be mean, but like I said before, it was bone-head English where students learned about punctuation use, highlighting, and various approaches to writing a paper. Also, using me, using a resource available to him, that sneaky man showed the class how to find resources available to them: sometimes that was me. Now that I think about it, that is kind of how I live my life. It is pretty much second-nature for me to examine all the possibilities and use the ones that work.

So, with all of this rambling about Rob and how he used me, basically as a teaching tool, you may be thinking, "What the heck did *I* get out of the class?" Well, think back on my first day when people couldn't get far enough away from me. Slowly, a few people at a time began arriving early to class to sit next to me and talk to me: not just questions about assignments but just chit-chat and getting to know me. So what did I get out of class? I got friends, and I got to begin my new journey of being "not the other" and part of a whole, just one of the gang.

I have to say that most of my college experiences were good, even great. Once the instructors and professors got to know me, understand my CP-babblistics, and we figured out how to accommodate testing and such, all was pretty normal. Yes, I just said that! College life was normal!

Besides Robert Sledge I had a few other favorites, ones that I especially connected with for some reason. There was Dr. Carroll, whom I called the Robin Williams of the English

Department. He always wondered why no one but me ever got his jokes. And talking about using resources . . .it wasn't until after I defended my Master's thesis that I confessed to him about how I learned the paragraph from Chaucer's *Wife of Bath* to recite, as was required for class. From my books on tape, I made my own tape with the loop of that paragraph about three dozen times. The confession didn't stop there. I also shared that that tape went from my hand to another classmate's hand, to another, to another, and to another . . .until I knew not where it was. Dr. Carroll wasn't even mad. He laughed and said, "Now I know why so many people recited the *Wife of Bath*. That's called using your resources!"

Another professor, Dr. Marshall, was on that list because she also accepted me as just another student. Well, in fact, maybe, I believe she thought I was, I don't know, gifted or had a canny knack for deciphering symbolism and underlying meanings in such literature and writings as George Elliot's *Middlemarch*, which I loved, by the way, and Shakespeare's *Othello*—so much so that I was generally one of the first students she asked to give feedback or opinion on. I mention *Othello* because that's when I gave her an AH-HA moment. I'm not going to go through the whole thing, but I am going to say that I explained to her my interpretation of a scene she had never understood before. Because of that interaction, I began showing her my own poetry, in which I heavily make use of symbolism myself. One day, after reading some of my work, she asked me if I had heard of *Penumbra*, the campus art and literary magazine. I had not, and when I did, an instant love affair began. I'm not talking about just the magazine but about most all of the people involved with the project.

Penumbra is where I met the indescribable, in a good way, Rofiah Breen, the facility advisor for Penumbra. I also met Patricia Housh. She and I became, what I like to call, the "dynamic-diva-duo." We not only became instant friends but sort of became the faces of Penumbra. Both of those women not only lifted me up, but they helped, allowed, and pushed me to fly, and after reading my work, my poetry and short stories, they became absolutely blind to any disability I had.

In fact, I remember an instance one year when some class member suggested the book open from bottom-to-top and not from side-to-side like a regular book. I fought so hard against the idea because, in my mind, it sucked, and it was totally wrong. I was so very-badly losing the fight on what I thought was a f#%*$-up idea that I pulled the "disabled card," saying something like, "I can't turn the pages on a book like that. How do you expect other disabled people to?" After class, both Rofiah and Patricia gave me nothing but grief, exactly as they would anyone. They laughed at me; yes, they laughed at me and said, "I can't believe you pulled the disabled card."

I answered, also while laughing, "I do what I have to do. Sometimes I just have to use my own resources." The two of them gave me no slack over that, again, as they would anyone, and made fun of me about it for months. Obviously, I deservedly earned it. This relationship lasted for years, like way after Patricia and I graduated with not only our Bachelor's but also with our Master's Degrees. We are still, to this day, connected, often speaking on the phone or via Skype. Cute story here: Rofiah became a grandmother a few years back. From day one, Rofiah would read to her. These readings included my books since Rofiah had bought all of them for her granddaughter as a Christmas gift. In fact, she bought two copies of each so she could read to her over Skype and Abby could follow along with her own book. Interestingly, my mom used to do that for my nieces and nephew, her grandkids. Anyway, at some interval, Rofiah mentioned she knew the author, Jennifer Kuhns. Abby requested to talk to "Jennifer Kuhns" and would not accept anything less. Well, we did talk via the internet in a three-way conference call: Abby and her dad, Rofiah and me. She asked all kinds of questions including why I was in a wheelchair. But the part of the conversation that I particularly enjoyed was Abby scolding her grandmother about my proper name. Rofiah of course, as all my friends do, called me, Jenni. Abby wasn't having that. She stated that my name was not Jenni but Jennifer Kuhns as was written on every book she had and, in so many three-year-old words, insisted I receive due respect. We still laugh about the seriousness of her opinion and attitude.

 My point in describing these relationships, why these professors were, what should I say here without sounding like an ass or presumptuous, drawn to me, I guess, was not because I was different. It was because I was capable. Okay, it may have initially been because I was different and may have sparked the tiniest bit of curiosity as to why this wheelchair bound person was in a university class at all. But in the same way I was an oddity, different, when I entered kindergarten, so it was when I entered college with most of the professors and students as well. My mental capability far out-shone my physical dysfunction.

Speaking of physical dysfunction, I bet you are wondering about something I haven't mentioned yet . . .testing. Testing was, besides being a pain, pre-arranged with each professor. Since most testing and exams were somewhat lengthy and I had to verbally respond to the questions so that my mom could put it to paper, bluebook, or Scan-Tron, (remember, she was my aide) I was provided an office, a spot in the library, or some other pre-determined area. If the test was a short quiz, I took it along with my classmates in the classroom. Kind of not a big deal for anyone—me or accommodations for me—until I had the distinct misfortune of meeting, hummm . . .I'm going to call him Dr. Dick, because he was. And I'm not saying this only from my perspective but from pretty much all the students in that class. (Now that I think about it, if he came up in conversation, most everyone had the same opinion of him as I did.)

The first instance that arose that influenced my opinion of the man was the weekly quiz about the assigned reading. The quiz was explained to be ten questions having to do with the storyline, theme of the book. He would be asking his chosen questions, and the class, as a whole, individually, would write their answers on a sheet of paper. After completing the quiz the class would correct their own papers. Easy, right? The honor system in place and all that. Except for me. Dr. Dick took me and my mother/aide aside and informed us that in place of the ten-question quiz, because I had to talk to my mom and someone might overhear my answer, I would be required to write a two-page paper referencing the storyline of the book . . .every week: in essence, a book report. I think we did that once. My mama-bear mother called "Bullshit" and confronted the man about the inconsistency of his plan: ten-questions verses two-pages. His next idea was to have me go outside and sit in the hall to answer the ten questions. I also did that only once, as well, before my mom put her foot down again and ushered me to my desk for the quiz and stated that I would be taking the test from there with the rest of the class.

I'm not sure if he was prejudging me, didn't know what to do with me, or was just an ass (I kind of think the latter). We all, not just my mother and I but my entire class, saw that I was being treated unfairly. The class thought so much so that they set the man up. It went something like this:

> There was to be a group presentation on . . .some book . . .I don't even recall what book it was at the moment. My group, as a whole, decided that I would be the presenter. I also have to reveal that at this time I asked my mom to step out of the room because I knew what was

possibly going to go down and I didn't want her help or involvement. She was confused by my request but complied and watched the goings on through the window from outside. When I began my dissertation on my group's findings, beliefs, and understandings of the novel, Dr. Dick was, shall I say, 'uncomfortably surprised' that the group had chosen me as there speaker. He continually interrupted me and did everything he could do to ignore and shut-me-up as fast as he could. In an effort to not talk to me, Dr. Dick attempted to address his questions to other people in my group. They, of course, had their own attack strategy. (It was like they had planned it.) When he asked, they replied with "Jenni just said that." After his several attempts to bypass me altogether, the group just opened up and blasted him with their own questions. "Why can we understand her every word, and you can't? Why do you always negatively excuse, exclude, and ignore her like her opinion has no value?" He answered with, "I didn't realize I was doing that." The class went ballistic and in total unison SCREAMED, "Excuse me! You have to be kidding! You always do this to her. Why are you doing it again?" My class had my back. They kept going at him with jabs about his condescending attitude towards me. He had no chance to respond, and I saw him, deservedly, in my mind, go from high and mighty to quiet and meek.

Actually, I did not return to the last day of class because the reading of *Penumbra* was on that day the following week. Nor did anyone else, for that matter. And after all of that, I found out from a fellow classmate that the man complained to her, complained, mind you, that I was an "overachiever" . . . like it was a bad thing. This is something I will inevitably and forever own because to this day, I always have to be better to be considered equal. On my final project for the class, though, he wrote these comments:

> As is often true, yours is the most complete, thorough,
> and thoughtful work I received.
>
> You should think about developing materials like
> this as a career.

I found his comments more than bizarre, considering how he had treated me and how he talked about people with disabilities in general.

And, come to find out, I was not the only one. After talking to students who had him as an instructor in other classes, I discovered he had made reference to his beliefs and attitudes—that those with disabilities were nothing more than a burden on society—and he couldn't understand why others didn't share his opinion.

Actually, a friend of mine who also has CP—not as severe as mine—had classes with Dr. Dick as well. One day, over coffee, she shared with me her experiences with him and her thoughts and feelings about his treatment of her. These are her exact words:

> He treated me like a second rate citizen, he was very unprofessional, rude, and very insensitive, and admitted he had no empathy at all for people with disabilities . . .until he had his daughter.

Are you ready for the B-I-T-C-H in me to come out? Not only did I write a letter against his tenure at the university because it was my feeling that someone with and who verbalized his prejudiced attitude should not be teaching (which didn't seem to influence those who hire and fire because he still holds his position as a professor), but fate also bit him in the ass. Shortly after beginning my Master's program, I found out he now had and was raising a special-needs child. Funny how what goes around comes around . . .God does work in mysterious ways, doesn't He?

A little harsh . . .okay, a lot harsh.

I need to back-up a couple of years. I had to put up with Dr. Dick for part of my sophomore year, and then I had no real contact with him for the rest of my two years on campus as an undergraduate student. Strangely, my first day back on campus for my first class as a graduate-student, Dr. Dick was the first person I saw and was the first person to welcome me to graduate school. I said thank-you, and that was the end of that. It was a little weird to say the least. I initially assumed he had seen the letter I had written against his tenure and was trying to kind of throw it in my face that he was still there. But that wasn't it. I think he was trying to . . .I don't know, mend fences. A few weeks after that brief exchange of words is when I discovered the existence of his infant daughter, a child with a disability. So yes, God does work in mysterious ways. I was humbled. I believe Dr. Dick had also been humbled.

One more exasperating example of the less than positive experience I had while at CSU Stanislaus was with a wonderful woman, whom I'm going to call Dr. B. She was one of those professors who had forgotten more than most of us will ever know in our lifetime combined. Since I had previous contact with her before I took one of her classes, I knew she was well accepting of me. But when I became an actual classroom student of hers there seemed to be a shift in her response to me. As with Dr. Dick, she would ask a question of the class, and I would offer my answer. She would never shy away from calling on me but rarely accepted my response. Most times she would either give a hummm . . ., move on to the next student for an answer, say nothing at all, or give her own interpretation of whatever it was she asked. At that point, someone in the class would give the exact same answer as I had just given or say, "She just said that." Dr. B. would then just look out at the class and say, "OH." None of us could understand why she didn't understand me, until . . .wait for it . . . she got her hearing aids.

Why am I telling you these stories? Because during my extended scholastic career there were sucky people or experiences intertwined with the good, but luckily there were fewer sucky ones than good ones. I suppose I'm trying to show that life is that way, as well. There is bound to be a little bad with the good—not just for those who are disabled but for everyone . . . so deal. It might sound cheesy, but to quote Forrest Gump, "Life is like a box of chocolates. You never know what you are going to get." I'd say be a candy-pincher to see what is inside: see what is available out there for you as a disabled person or . . . not. Don't settle for or be satisfied with what you are offered, if it, whatever it is, is not what you want or need. Be your own advocate. Write your own letters. Surround yourself with supporters who stand behind you and hold you up.

You may not believe me since I have pretty much only talked about school, going to school, and school related activities, but I did have a life outside of school. I referenced, earlier in the book, that my mom became my (and still is) IHSS Care Provider when I turned eighteen years old. She had had a career, before kids, as a registered dental assistant. When my siblings and I came along, let's just say things changed, and she stumbled upon a job that was a better fit for our family, time-wise anyway. She became a waitress. She has always said that she made as much money, if not more, as a waitress than a dental assistant, and she, as funny as it may seem, really enjoyed that job. Anyway, when it became apparent that, because of time and circumstances, I would need her to accompany me to college as my aide (which she initially hated, BTW), her world, our world, our relationship went through a major-shift. One of those major-shifts, other than figuring out who was the boss and who was not at any given time, was the idea that my mom was no longer going to be working outside of the home . . .other than with me.

Another thing I realized many moons later was that my mother thought it was very important to, what she called, "get me out in the world, out and about." What she really meant, what her real goal was and still is (I guess I say that a lot), was to help me experience and be part of life outside of home and school. While at school, high school, or junior college, or school-related social events, I was always in my element, but as I moved away from those familiar home-town people and places, it wasn't so easy or comfortable.

Now that I think about it, my dad used to do the same thing when I was little. He called it "airing me out." I think I called it, "giving Mom a break." Whatever anyone called it, I think it was their way of exposing me to the world and the world to me. And so began the idea of networking!, which, if you aren't aware, sometimes for a disabled person is doable but takes so much longer . . .for so many reasons.

Back to my mother making sure I experienced life as a full-fledged college student with me in the driver seat . . .maybe still with more than a tiny bit of guidance or overruling on her part. I have to share this: In the study of English or literature, there is a term called point-of view or who is narrating or telling the story. The abbreviation for that is POV. When my mom didn't agree or approve of some choice or decision I made, she would say POV. The thing was, she didn't mean point-of-view. Ya'll gotta know what that stands for, right? Someone you know has had to have watched Big Brother at some point. She, in code, was letting me know a later conversation would be had with the translation of POV. (power-of-veto)

Dang, I'm so far off track, again! My point was going to be that we did things and attended things in the community: like the time we went to a Mark Wills concert at the old State Theater in Modesto, the next biggest town near us. I loved Mark Wills at the time.

During his show he sang a song titled, *Don't laugh at me*. It's a song about . . .well here are some of the lyrics: *Don't laugh at me, don't call me names . . .In God's eyes we're all the same, Someday we'll all have perfect wings . . .Either in my head or because it was a live show and he may have changed the wording, I heard " . . .We'll all have unbroken wings."*

Now, I'm going to take you back to my mom's infamous POV, but first a little back story. For several years I had wanted a tattoo. I didn't know what kind or of what, but I so wanted one. HER, my mom . . .as in the major ruin-er of all things . . .even though I was twenty-three years old, a totally legal age to get a tattoo, said no. Wait, she didn't actually say no. She wanted to know what I wanted to get a tattoo of. And oblivious me, I had no idea; I just wanted a tattoo 'cause I thought they were cool. My mother quickly response, like she had practiced her answer. She simply said, "I'm not saying no to a tattoo. I'm saying no to a tattoo just because you want some ink like everyone else. It should have some kind of meaning or significance to you. When you figure out what that is, get back to me."

That night, as we listened to Mark Wills sing that song, I not only knew what tattoo I was going to get, but I could also tell by the look on her face that my mom knew I had found my tattoo, as well. In the crowded, noisy theater I tried to convey to her my epiphany. She couldn't even hear me and surprisingly answered with a head shake and a YES. After the concert, as we walked and rolled to our car, I started to ask or tell her again about my tattoo-thought. I barely even got started before she interrupted me with "That is exactly what I was talking about. A pair of broken-wings is perfect."

It was only a week or so later that my dear, dear mother took me to get my 'first' tattoo. I would have gotten it much sooner, except it proved to be difficult to get any—and this is the funny part—male tattoo artist to touch me, much less give me a tattoo. My mom must have called a half- dozen tattoo parlors to get an appointment, but when she explained that I had cerebral palsy and was in a wheelchair, the response was the same. "I don't feel comfortable doing that." Not willing to give up, my mom called and finally connected with a woman named Alana. After listening, once again, to her go through her rehearsed speech, I realized that she had gotten a different response from the 'woman,' because my mom said, "Really?" I could hardly wait for her to hang up and share with me what had just transpired on the phone. Long story short, and I can so feel you shuddering at the thought of what I'm going to say right now . . .probably in disapproval . . .the next afternoon I was sitting inside Main Street Tattoo getting my set of Broken Wings tattooed on my left shoulder.

I was ecstatic when it actually started to happen. A little setting and back story is probably necessary here. Remember me noting earlier that my mom was a registered dental assistant? Well, part of that profession includes knowledge and the practice of sterile procedures. When we walked in the building, the place smelled of bleach and other cleaning supplies—which was a plus in the establishment's column for my mom. Then when Alana took the sketch we had come up with and made a carbon copy of it and set it on a sterile drape, she scored another point. Alana prepared the area on my shoulder to be tattooed as my mom scrutinized every technical and sterile move she made, approvingly. Then it happened . . .I could see my tattoo flying out the window . . .Alana dropped the carbon copy of my broken wing drawing ON THE FLOOR! Did you just gasp? Ha ha . . .My mom did not. She said not one word. Instead my mother eagle-eyed Alana as Alana kicked that copy to the side and yelled for someone to please make her another as she opened the steri-pack of instruments she would be using. Obviously, Alana had passed my mom's test, and by the end of that afternoon I was sporting the first of, let's just say, a few tattoos.

    As a bit of a side-note: when people became aware of my new addition, not my peers, but, how do I say this?, the older-than-me generation were sort of appalled—not at the tattoo but at the idea of my mother not only allowing me to get one but actually taking me to get it. She was never phased by others' reactions. She spoke her mind and relayed her thoughts on the subject. What she said was this, and it pretty much shut everyone up:

> First of all, she is twenty-three years old and can legally get a tattoo if she wants one. Secondly, if she could have figured out how to get there by herself, she would have. By me taking her, I got to see for myself that there wasn't sawdust on the floor and spittoons in the corner. I'd rather be there and see for myself than find out later that there was some back-alley shit going on.

You may be wondering why I spent so much time on tattoos. I know it isn't a normal or expected conversation when discussing disabilities or people with disabilities. As silly and strange as it may seem, the truth of the matter is that tattoos are a big part of my life. Why?, you may ask—Well, because it is my way of commemorating an important event or achievement in my life, as well as some of those who have ahold of a large chunk of my heart. I have one for each book I've had published. I also have one that represents my sister, my brother, my two nieces, and my nephew.

My second tattoo was a no-brainer. When my sister asked me to be in her wedding as a bridesmaid, I almost said no because I didn't want to ruin it for her. I didn't want the spotlight on me. I wanted it on her, where it was supposed to be. She assured me that she would not have asked me if she didn't want me to be up there with her. She made a comment about me standing up with her (even though I don't physically stand: that whole metaphoric thing) . . .and it hit me. She was wearing white ballet-slippers with her wedding gown as a precautionary measure because, since she didn't wear dresses or heels often, she was afraid she would trip or something and fall on her face . . .for real; and, as I said, it hit me. That would be the perfect tattoo to represent our relationship and this occasion.

After the celebratory weekend, I was again in front of Alana getting a tattoo of a pair of ballet-slippers on my right-upper-thigh. That one was a short time later followed by a football.

The next big occasion in my life was when I completed my Master's program and, on April 29, 2008, defended my Master of Arts thesis-project at a meeting with my Master's committee members, who I made tell me twice that I was no longer in graduate school but was . . . done . . .a graduate! All that was left for me to do was 'walk,' which I did in May, a day I would share with Patricia and a few of my other *Penumbra* posse. I felt especially proud and honored when they called my name, and, as I accepted my diploma, a rush of professors, almost all the professors I had had over the last seven years at CSU Stanislaus, my professors, surprised me by stampeding onto the stage, almost running my mother over in the process. They flash-mobbed me with hugs and that-a-girls until there wasn't a dry eye in the place, mine included. I realized I was going to miss these people and this place that had become a big part of my world. After the fact, though, I realized that I was being a tad short-sighted in how I was going to be spending my time over the next couple of years. It was not even two weeks later when my first niece was born and my days became busier than I could have imagined.

    I thought after graduation my life was going to slow down. I mean I had spent most every day either on campus or somewhere doing homework. I thought if I had no school I'd have nothing to do, and life would be boring and lonely. This isn't a poor-me statement. Unless you have any connection or contact with the world of disabilities, you might believe it was. In reality, a stagnant life is more common than you'd think among the disabled community. For me for the last twenty-six years—basically my entire life, my every waking-moment had revolved mostly around scholastics and school-related activities. I was actually a little afraid I'd be stuck at home in front of the TV for days, months, and years at a time, with no interaction with the world, no goal or objective in my sights to strive for. Boy, was I wrong. My mom and I did take a couple of days to veg-out, and that is all it took for us both to get bored.

Prior to graduation, we did sneak in a few 'baby-shopping trips,' but now, after we took our breather, we were ready to go at it full-force. We had to be fully prepared for baby-sitting duty. We actually didn't start officially babysitting for several months until my sister went back to work, but we saw my niece (oh, and my sister) almost every day. The rest of my time was spent sitting in front of my computer or at Starbucks researching publishing houses and writing query letters to publishers, a somewhat daunting task. Okay, so Starbucks is a hub of socialization, as well. So I keep up with friends and gossip. It was never all work. Did I mention that my thesis-project was my first children's book? Yep, my first book was complete in April of 2008, but it wasn't published until 2010. So, basically it took me two years of talking, meeting people, drinking way too much coffee, and networking to find a publisher who would take me on. That was my summer.

In the fall I was no longer worried about being bored or gazing blindly at a television screen all day—far from it. We babysat Monday through Friday, six hours a day.

Also, shortly before the school year started, Rofiah had contacted me about *Penumbra*. No, I was no longer enrolled in school, but she requested my help, along with Patricia's, as it turns out, for multiple years after we'd graduated and left the university. On top of that, I finally found a publisher to publish my first book! That was more work than I had ever anticipated but well worth the effort and time. I'm not going to go into the process because it would feel like I was poking you with a chopstick in the arm over and over and over until you couldn't stand it and wanted to punch someone. Trying to explain the process would be overwhelmingly dull, unless, of course, you were interested in the world of publishing. Case in point, my first book, as I said earlier, *Were You Born in That Chair?*, took two whole years to get onto bookstore-shelves. In other words, it was a very long but satisfying journey, so satisfying that I jumped right into my next book, what I call a companion to *Were You Born In That Chair?: A Box Full Of Letters*. That book would take me two years to write.

Although writing had easily become my . . .shoot, I don't know if I'd call it my profession, but I'd definitely call it my passion and what I did on a daily basis (kind of like a job), I continued to also have life experiences. For example, in the summer of 2009 (the day after my niece's first birthday, BTW), my parents and I left on an extended road-trip to Tennessee, Michigan, and Iowa. You may have noticed that I didn't call it a vacation. That's because the first two stops were more of a meet-and-greet kind of a thing. Iowa was a known-entity, family and relatives I had known like forever. That part of the trip was the vacation part. Another long story short, a couple of years earlier my mom had discovered and contacted brothers she didn't know she had. Weird, right? Anyway, timing, health, and a variety of other variables finally came together, and we were all going to meet.

Off track one more time here. Have I mentioned that my wheelchair—my main wheelchair—is electric? Well it is. It is the one I use on a daily basis. But there are those occasions where some place or some building is not ADA-compliant (American's with Disabilities Act of 1992); they were grandfathered-in by law as exempt, for some reason. The reason I bring this up now is because I also have a manual wheelchair, what I call my push-chair which I use in those non-ADA situations. The crux of this whole discussion about wheelchairs is about our decision to only use my manual-chair on the trip. I was not a fan of that decision in the beginning. I hated the thought of being dependent on someone else for my every movement. Well, come to find out, almost every single house in the Mid-West is at least two stories! Imagine that! Maybe my parents knew a little something about where we were going and what was needed, after all. I was lucky they didn't cave to pleading and angry fits to take the electric. (I'd never tell them that, of course.)

Back to meeting new people, new family members. Remember my initiation to a new world, a new town, a new school, and new classmates in Rob Sledge's class: the one where the people in the class were faced with something they were unfamiliar with and opted to move as far away from me as they could in order to steer clear of any possible contagious element (which is not an all-that-odd or abnormal reaction I have found over the years, at least from adults in California)? Grandiose statement I know, but believe me, it is true. I know from experience. Years ago, while visiting my mother's grandparents in Kentucky, while in a Piggly-Wiggly (I kid you not, for real, Piggly-Wiggly), from out of nowhere, a woman came up to my mom and asked, "What's wrong with that baby?" I know exactly what the woman said because my mom has told that story a million times. My mom was absolutely stunned and speechless. When she tells the story she also states, "I couldn't believe that woman was so brazen as to just walk up to me and ask that." Then she shares that, after thinking about the interaction for a minute, she actually found it refreshing that someone would not just side-eye stare at me but point-blank ask what she wanted to know. The end result . . .my mom kind of liked it. And not to generalize, but I'm going to. People from the South or Mid-West seem to have a different attitude and acceptance-level towards . . .gosh, how do I say this . . .an open-mindedness about "things" they don't understand or that are unfamiliar. Living in California I find that people tend to shun and pretend you don't exist. The exception to that rule is people who know someone disabled (and who knows how that happens?), have a disabled family member, or work with disabled people. Those kinds of people are not afraid to approach you—me—a disabled person. Okay, sort of rant over. Where was I? Oh, ya . . .

The first new family members we met were my mother's uncle, aunt, and one of her brothers, all of whom live in Tennessee. Nothing but awkward is what I thought the entire day was going to be about. The awkwardness, though, lasted for like 3.2 seconds before my mom's aunt said, "Ya'll get yourselves in here and cool off with some sweet tea." No stares. No explanations. No "What's wrong with her?" It was like they had known me my whole life and not just for five minutes. Throughout the day, more people showed up to check-out the family from California: none of them tripped up a bit at the sight of me; rather, each and every one of them took me into the fold very quickly. In fact, one of my favorite memories of that first day in Tennessee happened that evening when the bunch of us went out to dinner. Wait, I should stay in the Southern-Mindset because it rocks: supper—we went out to supper. So while my dad was looking for a handicapped parking space, we made several trips around the parking lot. Dad finally found a handicapped parking spot close to the front door of the restaurant. As he pulled our big 'ole van into the space, my mom's uncle sauntered over. A little frustrated, my mom looked at the car parked in the handicapped spot next to us that had no placard or plate to be seen, as a woman entered said-car and flippantly asked, "Do you think all these people in the handicapped-spaces are handicapped?" To which (I'm claiming the man as my own now) My Great-Uncle looked right at that woman and replied loud enough for her to hear, "Ya, in the head." The man definitely had a full-fledged handle on something I call handicapped-humor.

Our next stop was in a place called Owasso, Michigan, where my mom, dad, and I met my mom's two other brothers. Again, I braced myself for a California—I'm calling it a 'response,' because in California it isn't a 'welcome.' But, once again, it was like they had known me my whole life, too. At a gathering with my new-to-me family one evening at the home of one of my uncles, we all started together in the back yard on the deck with a meal. As the evening wore on, little by little, person by person, the bulk of the group had moved downstairs to the finished basement where the music and real partying was getting started. You see, one uncle is a DJ, one uncle used to be in a band and still rocks a mean guitar, one cousin sings, one cousin dances . . .well, when they all get together it all happens together. Where am I going with this? Ah—wheelchair—downstairs in the basement. I was sure I was going to be left out and to my own entertainment with whomever was delegated to stay up top and babysit me. I tell you what, I love being wrong.

That Southern hospitality has a long, long reach, smothered in the idea of inclusion. I know, Michigan really isn't southern, but you get where I'm going, right? Tennessee-Michigan . . .Anyway, to the absolute horror of my mother, my two uncles and a couple of male cousins decided that they were going to carry me downstairs to the basement in my wheelchair. The kicker was these guys, or most of them, are firefighters and carry non-mobile people out of burning building just that way, all the time, in chairs. Another side note: Had I had my electric chair—the one that weighs five-hundred pounds, the one I whined over not being able to bring—I more than likely would have been left-out, upstairs, and to-my-own entertainment with whomever was delegated to stay up top and babysit me. Or someone would have really hurt themselves trying to include me. Not that it gave any comfort to my mother, but someone did tell her that they did this all the time. It was part of the job. I remember hearing her say to them, "Ya, but you drop her and you are still dead." The uncles and cousins are obviously good at their job. We all lived.

The next leg of our trip was to Iowa. I have to pause here to think, because this part of my family I have known almost since the day I was born. The truth be told, my father's cousin was a nurse at Stanford, the hospital where I was born, and she met me almost as soon as my dad did. I've been told that that's why my middle name is her first name, because she was the first person to see me. I guess what I'm getting at is that there was never any thought as to how I would be accepted. I had been since day one. Besides that, there was a full circle kind of thing happening as well. My namesake had a younger sister who had Downs Syndrome, so a child with a disability was not out of the ordinary for them. Also, my namesake's father, my great-uncle B. was one of the founding fathers of the organization, Camp Courageous. They were all about inclusion, loving for the sake of loving and in it for the long haul.

When we returned home from enlarging our familial circle, I settled into, not a grind, but a working-routine, I guess. I was determined to get the manuscript of *Were You Born In That Chair?* published. After hours and hours and hours of networking, I finally found a publisher who was willing to publish my book. I came upon Major and Shalako Press through one of those schmoozing—a-friend-of-a-friend kind of things. Actually, Major was really more than willing. He seemed genuinely excited about publishing it. I remember him saying that he believed the subject matter of the book was one "of great importance." It was a subject that hardly anyone, *if* anyone, had addressed in contemporary children's literature, and it needed to be. Did you hear that? "Great importance." I had always thought so, myself, but then again, my opinion was probably considered a wee-bit biased.

So for the next few months I went to 'the office,' better known as Starbucks, and edited, worked with the illustrator, came up with a cover design and all kinds of other little details that seem to manifest themselves while publishing a book.

A blast from the past kind of story just popped up and deserves explanation. I mentioned 'the office,' a kind of non-descript . . .place, space, building . . .whatever. One day when my mom and I were leaving for a day of writing or whatever we were doing that day, my dad asked, "You guys going to the office?" Seems like it should have been a fairly bland, maybe comical reference to what I called my work. The reality of it was that it was a reference to my grandfather who had died some eleven years earlier. He would go every morning, and sometimes in the evening, to a local restaurant to meet up with his trading, farming, or whatever-buddies, to as he called it, take care of business. What they really did was drink coffee and shoot the bull. Maybe my dad was ribbing me for how and where I spent my days, but I found it to be more endearing that he was remembering how we would make fun of my grandfather for going to 'the office' and that I was now doing the exact thing I would poke fun at my grandfather for doing. A fond memory . . .

In May of 2010, my first book was published and listed on several distributor's lists as well as Amazon. I had a book for sale on Amazon! Talk about flying high on cloud nine. I was absolutely stoked—so stoked that I got my first book-related, are you ready, yep, tattoo, with plans of a second. That's right. Even though I was determined to get my book, *Were You Born In That Chair?* published, our trip to visit new and old relatives sparked an interest in genealogy and inspired a second children's book. This second book, *A Box Full of Letters*, tells the story of a man traveling across the country to boot camp after joining the army in 1942 and revels what he encounters along the way. And therein lay the problem: although this man, in reality, was my grandfather from Iowa (my dad's dad), I knew basically nothing of the history, of the time, of the land, of the community, or of the man. That is where my scholastic training came in handy, believe it or not. Who would have thought I'd have to do research to write a children's book? But I did—and did lots of it. And a good portion of that research is included in the book even though the theme of the book is fully about discrimination and segregation. Anyway, in 2012, I got not one but two new tattoos. Along with *A Box Full of Letters*, I also wrote and had published a little story titled *Hailey's Dream,* about a young girl in a wheelchair who turns into a mermaid— sort of. I was on my way, if I didn't consider myself one yet, to becoming an author.

For some reason, mentioning mermaids makes me think of a mini-vacation my mom and I took with my brother, my sister, her husband, and my niece, who, at the time, was not quite two-years old. My dad volunteered to stay home with the five dogs that we had among the bunch of us. He seemed to think running a doggie-daycare was more of a vacation than going to Disneyland with the rest of us for my belated 30th birthday present. For most people this wouldn't seem to be worthy of space on the page or of even bringing it up in the first place, but this was to be my first-time visiting Disneyland and California Adventure Park. Remember, I was thirty years old, and for almost all of my life I had heard about and wanted to see the *It's A Small World* attraction. I wanted to ride the ride.

At this point you may be thinking, "What's the big deal? Just go." Remember when you had little kids and you had to pack up and take every damn little thing they owned when you went anywhere? That had not changed much for me at thirty . . .or even today at almost forty. Besides that, I no longer weighed twenty or thirty pounds, so picking me up and transferring me to some of the rides was not an easy option. Enter my big little brother who is over six feet tall and plays rugby: primarily, I should add, as something called a "Loose Head Prop" (a defined position on the pitch: one of the big guys who lifts another big guy). He was one of my 'every damn little things.' Anyway, besides being picked up, carried, too, and held-securely (by my brother) in the seat of the *Tower of Terror* ride, I also got to ride the *It's a Small World* ride all by myself, in my chair, in a special floating car made for wheelchairs following behind my mother, my brother-in-law, and my niece. I had no idea that places like Disneyland had (I hate this word) 'special' accommodations for folks like me. I came home with a ton of memories and a pair of Mickey Mouse ears.

If I were to keep things flowing in chronological order, something, if you noticed, I don't have the best handle on, right about now I should share that in 2011 I became an aunt again with the addition of a second niece. My consecutive thought process and recall tends to flow like life happens. I mean, who has one thing happen at a time apart from every other thing in their life. Anyway, shortly after my second niece was born we had a lightbulb moment, in an indirect way, because of her. All my life I have had various issues with clothing, most of which have been overcome. The one clothing issue my mother and I had yet to come up with a significant and workable solution for was pants. This is going to sound silly from the onset, but if you think about it, you will understand the truth of it.

To begin with, I had the unfortunate luck of inheriting what we Kuhns' call the Kuhns Curse. What is the Kuhns Curse you might be asking? The Kuhns Curse is more commonly known as A BIG German BUTT. Now add that to the everyday action of sitting. Okay, stay with me here and try and visualize as I try and explain. When one stands, one's pants are in perfect and pristine position. When one even begins to sit, one's pants begin to slowly creep down one's backside exposing one's plumbers attribute. In essence, your butt becomes bigger. Since I am always sitting I'm sure you can imagine what my pant issue is all about. Over the years my mom had taken on the task of making pants for me so all of my attribute would be covered, but style was never a concern for her. Besides that, there was so much more material, stiff and itchy around my midriff area that it tended to make me too hot, so it was never really a great fix. Enter niece number two and the shared idea of me wearing maternity pants! What?! Yep! Maternity pants was to be the perfect answer to the question, 'How does one easily pull a wheelchair-bound person's pants up easily and have them cover said butt-crack—again, I must say—easily as well as completely?' And you know every pregnant mama ain't wearing something that isn't 'stylin,' so the in-style style was right up this self-proclaimed diva's alley. Now-a-days, with the invention of yoga pants and the return of the 1980's leggings—which I had many of at the time—I have a butt-load (pun intended) of options to choose from. Of course, my options and clothing choices depend on where I'm going and what I'm doing on any given day.

 Somewhere between when my first book was completed and-on-the-market and 2012 when my second book was completed and-on-the-market, I began going to book fairs, sometimes with my publisher, sometimes as a solo-act. Obviously, I thought I had to dress the part of an author, whatever that was/is, and I had a multitude of looks before I figured out that it didn't make any difference what I wore as long as I was clean and presentable.

Speaking of publishing, book-fairs, and selling books, I feel it necessary . . . not maybe necessary but still totally gratifying . . . to say that, while sharing a booth or space with my publisher, I found that I was a way better salesperson than he was. Even his wife, who liked it when I sold books with him noticed and mentioned it. On more than one occasion she would say to me, "You are so good at this. Can you help him?" And then we'd laugh I told her that I had to accredit my approach to peddling my wares to a couple of things.

First of all, people do that "look-but-don't-look" thing when they see me . . .Y'know, "I saw you, but I'm going to pretend that I didn't" thing. So over time, I learned to take advantage of that split-second between the "I see you" and "I don't see you" to blurt out a single, simple word. "Hi." That lone word opens the door for interaction. For most people it would just be an ice-breaker or an attention-grabber. For me it is both an attention-grabber and ice-breaker, but also, more importantly, it's that 'startle' moment when they have to look. It draws people to the realization, the fact that I see, I hear, and I talk . . .I have abilities! This leads to the question, "Did you write these books?" And the conversation goes on from there.

Secondly, I have to give credit to my time as an FFA member and to my friend, Matt for giving me the advice and practical knowledge to not stop talking but speak my voice, push for acknowledgment, and not accept being ignored, and show that I can.

I sort of think speaking up and speaking our minds kind of runs in the family, like a personality-trait or something. Why do I say that? Well, because thinking about speaking one's voice and what-not reminds me of a time my mother and I were shopping with my sister and her three children at a Target. We were always our own circus train . . .lol. Anyway, my oldest niece needed to go to the bathroom, and my mom and I offered to take her so shopping wouldn't have to come to a complete stop. As we made our way to the bathroom (my niece sitting on my lap because she said that she was tired of walking) we approached a little girl sitting in the front of her grandmother's shopping cart. When the little girl noticed us, all of a sudden, in her loudest voice, she unabashedly hollered, "Grandma, what's wrong with that girl?" (Okay, maybe it's more than a family trait.)

Embarrassed, the grandmother attempted to shush the little girl by putting her hand over her mouth and whispering "shhhh." At that point my mom grabbed one of my business cards and offered it to the woman saying, "Maybe this would help you explain it to her." Now, understand that my niece was still in my lap taking in the goings-on. When my mom returned and we continued to make our way to the restroom, she stood up on my footboard, looked over my shoulder and indignantly asked, "What's wrong with THAT girl? There is nothing wrong with Aunt Jenni!" Of course, that too was spoken loud enough for the whole of the store to hear. As a side note: she was also pretty impressed and excited when she saw the handicapped emblem on the unisex/family bathroom door, expressing her delight by stating, "Look, there is a bathroom 'specially for Aunt Jenni!"

At the time I found this extremely funny, not just because of the obvious 'kids saying the darnedest things,' but because just a year before, a tad before her fourth birthday, she had an epiphany concerning me through a series of events in her life. Before my niece noticed I was different, the series of events went like this: First she went to the movie theatre and saw the movie, *Brave*. The significance of that movie is that the king in the movie lost his leg because a bear bit it off and he had a peg-leg.

The second occurrence that led to her insight was a few days later when she got a new preschool teacher who had a prosthetic leg. As kids do, she made the connection to the recently-seen movie and asked him if a bear had bitten his leg off. He of course, didn't make the connection and said, "No, why would you ask that?" She answered, by explaining the movie to him and about King Fergus getting his leg bitten off by Mor'du, the bear.

This brings us to the third and final moment when my niece figured out that there was indeed something a little odd, something different about me that she had not seen before: something she had actually seen since the day she was born, but never seemed to give it a second thought much less a first thought.

The weekend after the movie and meeting the new teacher, my dad, my mom, and I went to my sister's family's home for my niece's birthday party. When I was getting unloaded from the side door of the van via the hydraulic ramp/lift, something my niece had witnessed hundreds of times, I could see in her face that she was having a light bulb moment. As soon as the ramp hit the ground and I rolled off onto the driveway pavement, my niece handed her mom the bunch of bananas she was holding (why she was holding bananas, I have no idea) and bolted towards my mother and me. She, without pause, proceeded to ask my mom the question that I had been preparing myself to answer for four years. She wanted to know why I was always in that chair.

The funny thing was, I, at that time, had just finished the manuscript for *Hailey's*

Dream, a book about a little girl . . .well, here, just read the first paragraph of the book:

> Hailey Burke was a little girl in a wheelchair. She was in a wheelchair because she was born too early. Her brain didn't have enough time to grow all of the way, so some of it didn't work. The part that told her legs how to walk didn't work. So, Hailey used a wheelchair to get around.

That is how we explained it to my niece. I had come to understand through discussions with preschool and kindergarten teachers that that is all children that age want to know—just why—not the technical, medical, blah, blah, blah of scientific study or research . . .or whatever . . .just simply-why. And that was all and the end of it. I don't recall discussing it in the seven years since then.

I do, as everyone does from time to time, think back on conversations and interactions I've had with people, especially those I've had with kids. I tend to hold on to those as fuel or springboards for my children's books. Remember the one with the grandma and the little girl and how my niece was pretty impressed and excited when she saw the handicapped emblem on the unisex/family bathroom door—the one that was 'specially' for me? That particular memory hit me in the face one afternoon in 2017. It's a bit of a long story but, I think, well worth telling.

So one day after my mom had a training session with her trainer at the gym, she had to pee, which isn't all that unusual for her, so we ran into the locker-room. Ya'll have been there, right, or at least taken a tour of a health club in the month of January in contemplation of joining a gym at some point as your New Year's resolution? There is a section for changing clothes, a place for showering, and another area with individual stalls—including at least one large stall specifically designated for disabled folks like me for relieving oneself. What I'm getting at is that there is a place for everyone to do everything. Anyway, the unusual circumstance was that I needed to pee as well. Not to brag, but I tend to have the ability to hold it for an ungodly amount of time. I know, I know, don't get on my case. I understand that not voiding one's bladder when the urge hits isn't a good thing, but it is such an inconvenience to have to stop and go.

Now that you can visualize the room and the situation, back to the story. My mom, in dire need of a free-stall, dropped me off at the entrance of the locker-room and told me to "get yourself there" as she ran to a regular-size bathroom stall. (Important to know the size of the stall here because I really can't use a regular-size stall.) I was just getting to my mark when my mom came out of the stall and made her way to the sink to wash her hands. The important part of this story is that the handicapped stall was being occupied by a twenty-something, able-bodied girl who was carrying on a conversation with another girl in an adjacent stall prior to my mother and me even entering the locker-room. I didn't know exactly what she was doing in there, but she wasn't sitting. We waited for some time. My bladder said it was hours, but more realistically: maybe ten minutes. If I could have, I would have been doing the potty dance.

Giving way to frustration my mother and I left and approached the front desk and explained our dilemma. The woman at the front desk actually found the girl's actions and conduct unacceptable, particularly since the stall had a handicapped emblem on the door—one even my niece at four-years old knew the meaning of.

The front desk lady, my new knight-in-shining-armor, confronted the girl who was still in the handicapped stall when we returned to the locker-room. It was a basic "shit-and-get-off-the-pot" 'cause you got someone else needing this stall kind of scolding—with an added "This-ain't-a-dressing-room!"

Shortly thereafter, the girl emerged from the stall. She did not say a word. She did not make eye contact. She did not even acknowledge my presence in the room. She didn't even look in the mirror to sneak a peek at us behind her. I know because my mom watched her to see if she would. The one person she did say something to was her friend who exited her stall after we had entered the now-empty-handicapped stall. While I was peeing like a proverbial racehorse, not kidding, we heard the handicapped stall squatter (who had not been squatting) say to her friend, "Well, they just think they are entitled."

My mother, bless her heart (I've heard that Southern women say that to excuse themselves for speaking ill of someone else) yelled out, "You're damn right she's entitled to this stall. It's a fucking handicapped bathroom!" And there you have it. A teaching moment, maybe . . .or maybe not. It depends on how entitled the girl in the handicapped stall was, I suppose.

The next major thing, the next "big happening" in my life, was the move to Chico, California in the fall of 2018. (Just as an added bit of information, we woke up one morning about six weeks after our move, to the reddest sky I had ever seen. The Camp Fire was in its infancy of making history just a few miles down the road from where we now lived.)

It had been an exciting time. Prior to actually moving, we looked at dozens of pre-existing houses. As we did so, we had to take into consideration changes that would need to be made: such things as door-openings widened or moved altogether. We also had to figure out if any walls needed to be totally removed and if the width of the halls were sufficient for me to drive down in my wheelchair—not to mention having to determine if I could actually make the turn into any given room from the hall on my own.

And then there was the bathroom. Did it have a tub or a shower—because doing a tub on a daily basis was not going to happen. A little bit of TMI here: My mom was a competitive power-lifter, but getting me over and in and over and out of a tub every day was just asking for an accident to happen. My point being, I needed a stand-alone shower that was big enough, again TMI, that my mother, a shower-chair, and myself would fit into. Very early on it had been through trial and error that we discovered it was more time-efficient and productive for my mom and me to just shower at the same time. Odd, but it works for us then and still.

Months of looking at homes and realizing the added cost of any already existing home would increase significantly with the adaptions that I would need almost caboshed the whole deal: our moving. When we thought all was at a stand-still—like just in the nick-of-time—my parents finally got the opportunity to view some new-builds in town. The advantage of a new-build, as it was when we moved to a new-build in Hughson seventeen-years earlier, was the fact that there was the availability to make structural changes before the house was anywhere near completed. We were able to go in with the contractor and make the modifications needed to make the house fit our . . .okay . . .my needs.

Wait, I want to back up a second. All modifications and or additions to the new house were not 'all' for only my benefit. All my life, most of my daily care has been provided by my mother. Since I am almost forty, without giving her age away, I can safely say she ain't no spring-chicken. With that out in the open and squarely on the table, I can share that the addition of something called the XY Tracking System in my bedroom, along with the high-back dressing sling and Shower/Toileting Chair was a blessing.

So I keep talking about trying everything, giving everything a shot, and if it works—wonderful; if not—oh well, let's move on. I talk about taking advantage of one's resources. Keep in mind,

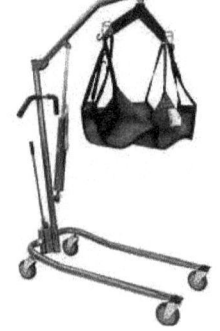

though, that while one is making use of any-given resource, the results or reactions will differ from person-to-person and may be logical or illogical, helpful or unhelpful, in each individual's case. I'm going to share a specific example of what I'm trying to convey.

Years ago we had a physical therapist from Kaiser come to the house to observe and evaluate my . . .let's say . . .needs as she saw them, and that is the key statement: as she saw them. She asked how I was transferred from my wheelchair to the bed to the toilet, and so forth. She was told that either of my parents would lift me from one place and carry and place me in another.

Well, that was absolutely appalling in her mind. To her way of thinking, neither one of my parents should be schlepping me around like that. She insisted the need for and ordered something called a Hoyer Lift fitted with a sling for me to use, she said, "from here-on-out." The idea was for me to hang from this frame-thing in the sling and then be pushed (while I swung back-and-forth and side-to-side) and be rolled over the bumpy tile floor to my end destination. Yep, that Hoyer Lift and Sling happened once, maybe twice, for thirty seconds . . .each time. It freaked me the hell out and scared the crap out of me to the point of tears. My reaction may have been illogical, but the fear was very real to me. The lift and sling ended up in the shed until we moved to Chico, when we returned it to where it came from, never-to-be-seen again. My parents, usually my mother, resumed and continued to pick me up out of bed, out of my chair, and on and off the pot for many, many years. Hence, the reason she took up powerlifting . . .to stay strong.

Had we not had that earlier experience, we might have been more accepting to the half-a-dozen family members who had, over the last few years, suggested the XY Tracking System/ceiling lift. My mom assumed, and I was just plain-assed convinced, it would never work. That's why, when we finally conceded to the idea of looking into the possibility of using this contraption, I was less than thrilled and basically did so in order to placate the rest of the world who was constantly bombarding me with a multitude of advertisements about the dang thing. This included my dad who had begun to push the use of the Hoyer . . .I want to say. . .due to the aging of my poor 'ole ma.

On one of our trips up to Chico, after first setting up an appointment with a guy from One Source Mobility (a company actually based in Chico, believe it or not), we went to test this thing out. This company manufactures and distributes the X-Y Tracking System among other handicapped-adaptive equipment. Saying that my mom and I were skeptical does not begin to explain how we felt. We were both absolutely positive the whole entire experience would be an exercise in futility and waste of everyone's time because it was not going to work.

Are you ready, and this is why you have to give every last little thing a try, after not tuning the guy out as he went over various configurations and systems and how the dang thing worked, he had us, my mom and me, give it a shot. He walked us through each step from getting the sling placed securely around me to lifting and transferring me to a shower chair and then to a set-up mock-bed and then back to my own wheelchair.

Holy Moly!!!! I don't know who was more surprised, me or my mom. There was not the slightest hint of a 'freak-out' on my part. On the other hand, my mom was more than slightly befuddled as to why I wasn't freaking-out. As true unbelievers would do, we ran through the process a half a dozen times or more just to make sure the first time wasn't a fluke and to give me a chance to freak-out if I was going to. My mom and I so wanted to say 'We told you so,' but we never got the chance because the darn thing worked like a charm. I later told my mom, in secret, by the way, that the reason I was okay with this setup was the fact that she was able to continually have her hand on me 'somewhere' (something I didn't realize I was in need of), and that provided me with a sense of security and trust I didn't have with the Hoyer (something else that I now obviously know I needed). It was that simple. Now I hang around in it, literally, just because it stretches out my back from hours of sitting, and it feels soooooooo good.

I should have learned that lesson a few years back when my dad found a hospital bed in the want ads and bought it because it was basically new (the man who was supposed to use it died before he had a chance). His justification was that I was going to probably need it at some point in the future and we weren't going to find one at such a good price when I did. Then he threw in that if I didn't need it he probably would.

Anyway, when he brought it home and set it up in my room, I wanted to cry. It looked like a sick person's hospital bed with fake looking contact paper wood headboard and footboard, big old chunky metal side rails and all that ugly hydraulic junk, wires and cords underneath needed for operational purposes. Ahhh, I had spent way too much time, thought, and energy on decorating my bedroom in a fashion that represented and fit the diva I thought I was to have him dump this thing in the middle of my world. Excuse me!

To my surprise, I don't know how, but my dad got it. He understood my less than ecstatic response to the bed. He began pulling pieces and parts off of the bed. I didn't really need a footboard. I don't think I had ever fallen out of bed, so the side-rails came off as well. Together we decided the headboard could stay because I could put some fancy throw or something over it . . .and all the junk under the bed. My mom made me an extra-large quilt that hung almost to the floor and hid it all. I was a happy little diva.

While we are on the topic of being a diva and having someone trying to tell me what to do or suggest that I should be doing something different than I am, like using a lift and a hospital bed and such, you'll notice it does not always sit well with me . . .and I tend to push back. Well, here is another time my dad tried to make me do something I didn't want to do—for my own good—mind you. Ya, that old line.

Let me explain. I had always slept on my stomach primarily because I had always felt like I was falling off the face of the earth when I lay on my back, even in bed, because, due to the cerebral palsy, I have no sense of equilibrium. Anyway, even though I had conquered my drooling issue decades ago and got my ears pierced as a reward (as promised and fulfilled by my dad, by the way), I still had issues with two things: moisture of any kind and me rubbing my face against my pillow, which caused a good-amount-of irritation. Because of this, I almost always had a rash or a rosacea sort of look to my cheeks. It is hard to look like a diva when it looks like your face is going to fall off at any moment. My dad, many times over the years, tried to talk me into sleeping on my back because he thought it might alleviate the problem.s And honestly, several times I tried. Those were some long and sleepless nights until I gave up and called my mom in the wee hours of the morning to flip me over onto my stomach again, and then I would fall right to sleep. Enter that ugly hospital bed that I didn't want in the first place with the controls that raise and lower one's head and/or feet. This new toy gave my mother and me the opportunity to play, as we usually did, when I got a new piece of equipment.

So, over the next week or two, we played with the control buttons and raised and lowered my feet, then my head—adjusting and trying different combinations until, believe it or not, I was comfortable, and sleeping on my back was no longer an issue. The reason? I'm thinking that, because the configuration of the bed—the mattress—was more like a chaise lounge and not flat, I no longer felt like I was falling off the planet when I lay on my back. You should see my soft as a baby's butt face now. I never did actually tell my dad he was right. I just sort of easily slipped into the habit of sleeping this way.

I never actually explained why we opted to move to Chico because, once again, I veered off-track. Well, it is pretty simple, really. My sister and her family lived in Chico. More to the point, it is where my two nieces and nephew dwell. They are kind of the shining lights in my life. I would do and go anyplace for them. We had already been coming up here for years because of birthdays, plays, school-performances, holidays providing another set of hands when one parent was out of town, and . . .well, any excuse to come up to see them. Besides that, they had been haranguing and harassing us to move to Chico for almost as long as they had been here.

A secondary bonus to moving in a northern direction is that it put my dad, mom, and me, half-again closer to where my brother and his girlfriend live. We are no longer five hours away, and we get to see them way more often than we used to. I call that a win-win!

Wow, it just dawned on me that my mother and father just recently went on their first outing, a date maybe, by themselves, without me since I don't know when. Turns out being in the same town as my sister has its upside for my parents, as well. Although I'm almost forty, I can't really be left at home alone and for all intent and purposes, need a babysitter, so to speak. I guess that makes it a win-win-win!

The scary part about moving to Chico and what could have been the down-side was the choice to leave the only medical insurance coverage I had ever known—Kaiser. My dad had had Kaiser for some time, like since the early 1970's, and my mom jumped on-board when they got married in March of 1978. It was a system we were all familiar with, and we knew what to expect, what it was going to cost us, what the insurance would and would not cover, and how things were done. What I'm getting at is that Kaiser was a known-commodity.

Since I, just a couple of paragraphs ago, told you I am almost forty, and don't forget, disabled, you may be wondering why my medical insurance carrier was not Medicare. Aaaaa, because we had Kaiser, and Kaiser my parents thought to be a better option than Medicare. Being born into the Kaiser "family," if you will, meant that "as long as I remained permanently-disabled, I would never be dropped or ejected from the Kaiser program or my parent's insurance plan" is what we were told. So it was a big step to leave the known for the unknown. Just as an FYI: we waited to move to Chico until my mom was old enough to join the ranks of Medicare, along with myself and my dad. All for one and one for all, y'know. The year that happened—when my mother made her sixty-fifth year around the sun—we took the leap, moved, and left Kaiser. As it turns out, it wasn't a bad leap. A little stressful, maybe in the beginning, but once we understood the program and the groove of how it all worked, it turned out to be a six-of-one and half-a-dozen of the other . . . so far.

Another downside to moving to a new city, town, or area is something I mentioned earlier. That something is networking.

Remember me saying sometimes for a disabled person, it takes so much longer . . . for so many reasons. Here I was doing it again. But after a little over a year I have made some connections, via, of course, Starbucks. When one sits in Starbucks for hours at a time, day after day, using it as one's office, one meets people, and talk and the networking begins. Oh, and my mom's connection or obsession with pottery and hooking-up with other pottery people, has been a tremendous help, as well. As a matter of fact, I've had a book-signing with the local Barnes & Noble and was asked to participate in a Christmas event at the same Starbucks where I write most of the time. This event is one that has taken place for several years, and Santa chooses and reads a Christmas-themed book each year. Guess whose book he is reading this year?

Did you guess? Your guess is only half-right. So, by the time this book is done and published, I will have nine books under my belt, one of which my oldest niece wrote with me. This is the part you couldn't have guessed. Let me tell you the story. About three-years ago now, when she was nine-ish, around Christmas time, she called me out about not having written a holiday, specifically a Christmas book. She, in all seriousness, asked me why I had not. I didn't have a good answer but did have an awesome lightbulb moment and comeback to her question. I admitted I didn't know why I hadn't written one and then asked her, "Why don't we write one together?" (I've been told I can be quick-witted.) You would have thought she had just won a million-dollars, got a new puppy and met Harry Potter in the flesh, all at the same time.

"Are you kidding me? Are you serious? You don't really mean it, do you? 'Cause if you are serious and do mean it, I have a story!" was her comeback without even taking a pause to breathe.

I laughed so hard I all but peed my pants, stopped breathing and had a flood of tears running down my face. When I eventually regained my composure, I addressed her stream of questions with, "Of course I'm serious. I wouldn't have asked if I wasn't."

"Do you want to hear my story?" was her next question. "'Cause it's all in my head."

"Absolutely, you bet I do. Let's hear it," was all I had to say.

Over the next thirty-minutes or so she proceeded to tell me the story she had titled, *Lilly Gets Lucky.* I'm not going to tell you anymore about the story. You'll have to read the book for yourself.

We spent the next year working together on the writing and illustrations. She actually hand-wrote the basic story-line and brought it to me so that I could expand or embellish or enhance her idea. She sketched out her ideas for the illustrations. When we got to the point of needing to do the book formatting and layout, she was part of the process and put her two cents in. Since she was doing the artwork and couldn't think of a "picture" for one of the pages I had blocked out, she asked if we could combine two pages so she didn't have to worry about it. "Sure, thing," I told her. I wanted to make sure she understood and was part of the whole process. Once we had all the parts: the writing, the illustrations (with the help of my mom/her grandma), and the formatting, we sent it off to the publisher. She was proud. I was even prouder. I haven't seen it yet, but a collection of stories is in the works. I take that back. I've seen the rough-drafts of the illustrations. I am immensely pleased that I could influence someone in that way, especially at that age.

Here I am close to the here and now: not the end of my story because I plan on doing, living, and accomplishing much more for many more years. I just don't know what that entails right now, so I can't share it with you. There is one thing I haven't mentioned much about. I haven't really delved into any medical issues or problems to this point, mostly because, other than cerebral palsy, I really didn't and don't have any "medical" problems. I've (knock-on-wood) been more or less heathy as a horse. I haven't been "ill" much in my life at all. I am betting that someday heredity will eventually catch up with me, but that is a whole other story. Yes, the CP has caused, I guess you'd call it, secondary conditions like having to wear glasses because of the transient-myopia, being on medication for a good portion of my youth because of a kidney-reflux, and what we all call "my spaz" meds . . .that which helps tame my startle-reflex. I do remember the three times as an adult or semi-adult that I got sick . . .in bed. Not that you want to hear the in-depth details about puking, but on my seventeenth birthday I learned that overindulging on your favorite food, mine being tortellini, is not a good idea . . . especially if you sleep face down on your stomach.

  After switching to sleeping on my back, the third time I got sick was (I'm skipping the second time because it was the same as the first) I can't really say easier or more comfortable, but it sort of was, but sort of wasn't at the same time. Instead of trying to hold my head up off my pillow in order to avoid snorting vomit up my nose, I was able to just turn my head and let fly . . .covering the surrounding circumference of my bed. This makes me think of the age-old debate about babies either sleeping on their stomach or their back and which is better. As someone who can vocalize the experience, I vote for back. There were, of course, more gross and gory details, but that is all I'm going to say about those events I'd rather forget.

On the other hand, most of my trials and tribulations in life have been more about my physical limitations and inability to perform the basic self-care and everyday living tasks. As my family and friends can attest, I have the ability to tell someone how to do something or preform any given task and verbally guide them through to-completion. I just don't have the capabilities (the manual dexterity, coordination, or control, I guess would be a better description of what I'm lacking) to do it myself.

Simple things that most people don't give a second-thought to, like feeding themselves, dressing themselves, turning a page of a book are things I need assistance with. Then there is going to the bathroom, wiping one's own butt, which pokes at your pride a bit and forces modesty quickly-out-the-window, never to return—all of which compels one to accept a certain amount of humility.

Still not a medical issue but one that every female has to deal with, usually on monthly-intervals, is the dreaded "visit." Again, not to be gross, but try getting one of those, I don't care what size they are, skinny-ass sanitary napkins to stay in the right place. I'm probably going to a TMI area here, but it is a real thing. And believe me, the other option isn't even an option for me, being as I am permanently sitting in a wheelchair.

For years my mom and I dealt with the mess of a mess as was traditionally done by every girl and woman on the planet. Then my sister, she who researches all things, brought to our attention something she had run across somewhere or other. She had read that an off-label use, as in more than one month consecutively, of birth control pills was a way around someone having monthly periods. After a doctor's visit and confirming her findings, I began taking birth control pills for three months running with a one-week break in-between. Having a period four times a year is way more manageable than twelve for my mother and me. That one week still sucks, though.

Then my mom came up with the "fabulous" idea of having me wear what we call paper underwear or adult diapers. Of course, I thought they were far less than fabulous when she first came up with the idea. I mean, why would anyone want to wear diapers. My brain automatically went to the "this is a punishment" kind of thing because if the truth be known, I've had my share of, what should I call it, maybe a mismanagement of time when it comes to alerting someone that I needed to use the facilities. Anyway, I wear them that one week every three months. I also sometimes wear them when we are on a long car trip, and even when there may be questionable bathroom accessibility. They are kind of a saving grace. They are an absolute stress-reliever and C.Y.A. addition.

Stumbling across the paper underwear was almost—sad to say—a gift of sorts. They aren't really considered adaptive or a modification of any kind for handicapped-use. They just happen to serve a workable purpose in my case. On the other hand, over the years there have been many pieces of adaptive or modified equipment that I have used or struggled to use that never worked for me. I've had buttons to turn on the television, swivel spoons to feed myself, page turner machines, to name a few, all of which were a bigger pain than they were worth. One thing that did work for me was having an adaptive, large button, slap-pad control land-line in my bedroom. In the world of cell-phones and blue-tooth technology, I am better off with an old-school table-top phone, designed for those with special needs, that I can verbally contact an operator with in case of a home-emergency.

Mentioning the doctor about getting conformation on the use of birth-control reminded me of a doctor's recommendations that went so terribly wrong. If you know anything about cerebral palsy, you know about muscle-contractures, a tightening or curling of pretty much all muscles. When I was an undergrad-student my neurologist suggested that I have a procedure done to loosen the muscles in my hands and wrists to enable me to have more control and dexterity involving my hand-function. She suggested that I have BOTOX injections, which were done just above my wrists. There was no surgery involved, so my parents and I decided to give it a try. Although maybe a tad skeptical, we decided to only do one arm at a time. This decision was both a good and a bad idea. I'm left-handed, and that was the side we chose to do first. The bad news was, I'm left-handed. In theory, I'd be able to use that hand better. But instead of making it better, the injection it made it worse. The muscle injected loosened up so much that my hand pulled back on itself, making it impossible for me to drive my chair at all. The good news? We only screwed up one hand and knew better than to do the procedure again. I did wear a brace on my left hand for a really long time to help rectify the bad result, but it never fully returned to the way it was before.

I suppose we could have gotten mad, but what good would that have done? One of my brother's favorite sayings is "It is what it is." What he means is, no matter what your feelings about something are, that is the "what" it is and your reality.

What do I feel about it? I've not always been happy about my condition, my situation in life. I've been mad, and I've been sad, and I've hated the body I'm in. I have literally looked at my hand and talked to it and yelled, "Come on, hand, work already!" All that being said, it doesn't change what is. What I do have in my grab-bag of skills is my mental-dexterity. I like to call it my convince-ability ability. I know how to harp like nobody's business to get what I need, want, or think I should have . . .not that it always works.

Over the years we have all learned to go with the flow. We tend to try everything and take suggestions. Sometimes all those things—the suggestions, the trials, the adaptions, the gadgets and devices we stumble upon—may work, and sometimes some may not, but you don't know until you try those things for yourself.

And there you have it, the highlights of my life in a nutshell thus-far. I hope, by sharing my story, I have been able to help you in some way and maybe shed some light on what is possible and do-able. If nothing else, I hope you have been entertained by this Broken-Winged Diva.

A final word . . .

Do you remember me telling you about testing out the X-Y Tracing System? Well, I thought I'd show you what I was talking about. So here's to not freaking-out!

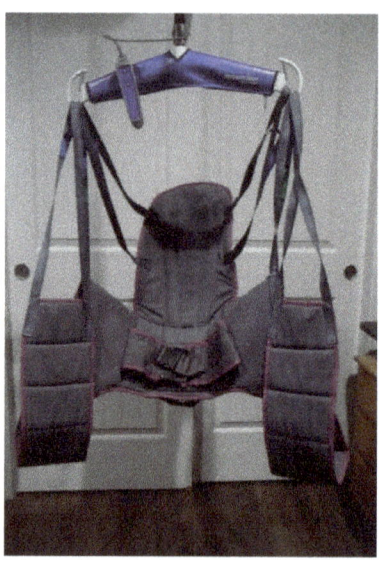 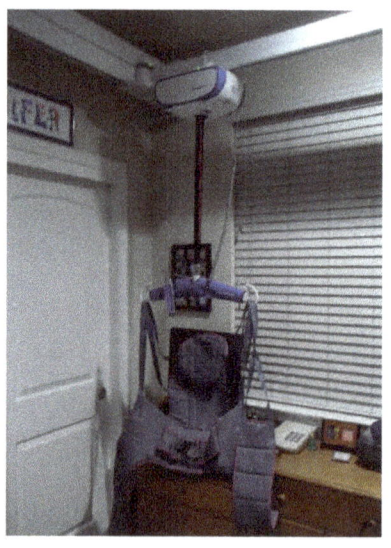

High-back shower/toileting sling with the accompanying X-Y Tracking System

It isn't the most gorgeous thing in the world, but in the here and now (probably should have been years before) it is the most beneficial piece of equipment I have. Well worth the cost.

Jennifer Kuhns

Sharing A Little-Bitty Brag Book

Even Broken-Winged Divas Can Fly

Sharing My Favorite Social Adventures

Meeting "Bo"

Jennifer Kuhns

Hanging with Daryle Singletary at FFA State Convention

In 1998: I had the honor of being nominated and winning the title of FFA Barn Dance Queen.

My second favorite show: *Survivor*
Meeting up with Ethan Zohn

A few of my proudest moments

Receiving our FFA State Farmer Degrees

My Reserve Champion FFA Market Lamb. (Remember the lamb from Colorado? This is that lamb.)

Even Broken-Winged Divas Can Fly

And Master of Arts Degree

Jennifer Kuhns

Four of my eleven book awards

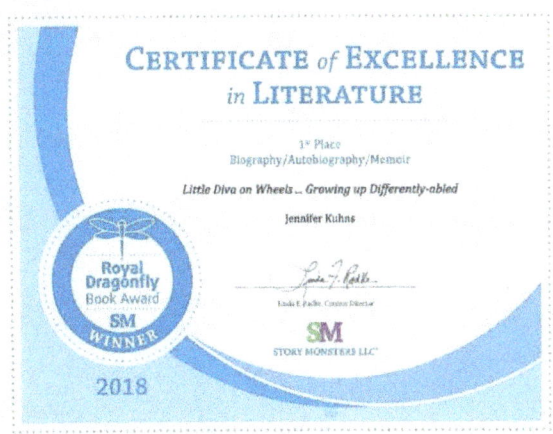

Making my mark on the world
. . .and my small claim to fame

Holding my own on the front page above-the-fold: the most desired-location in the whole paper.

Jennifer Kuhns

The Signal — April 2004

Artist learns publishing at campus magazine

Michael Arellanez
Signal staff

Perhaps it's her smile, her blue eyes or her charm, but after any conversation with CSU, Stanislaus student Jennifer Kuhns you walk away with a great impression of this painter and poet.

Growing up most of her life in Gilroy, California then moving to Hughson in order to attend CSU Stanislaus, most people would assume that her move would be a difficult transition. However, that's not the difficulty Jennifer faces.

Hughson is afflicted with Cerebral Palsy, a condition that affects the motor movement of the central nervous system. Though, by talking with her you would never guess that she's aware of her condition because her spirits are very high.

Cerebral Palsy can have an effect on speech, so Mitzi Kuhns, Jennifer's mother, spends Tuesdays and Thursdays with her daughter on campus sometimes translating for Jennifer. When not in class the both of them are running new jokes by each other.

"Laughing is what I think really can bring my family together," said Jennifer. Jennifer, who's bound to a wheel chair because of her Cerebral Palsy, jokes about why she chose to attend CSU, Stanislaus.

"When I was living in Gilroy I had some problems with my wheelchair. Before coming to CSU, Stanislaus I attended the Junior College in Gilroy which had a lot of hills to climb on campus, so I really

Photo Courtesy of Jennifer Kuhns

Taking the English class *Editing Literary Magazine* this spring has given Jennifer a better perspective of publishing. For a while she was unsure why her work was not getting published and what steps she should take to find a publisher. By taking the class many of her questions have been answered.

As part of the class Jennifer works on the *Art and Literary Magazine* known simply as *Penumbra*. It's an annual production of artwork and literary works combined to reflect the passion and talent of those whose works are published in the magazine.

Jennifer's artwork and poems that are published in this years *Penumbra* reflect

wanted to pick a campus that was mostly flat."

When not poking fun Jennifer spends her time painting and writing poetry. As an English major at CSU, Stanislaus she hopes one day to have her writings published into books for children. When she was a child one of her favorite books and the one that inspired her to write for children was *itsy Witsy Nitsy*. Currently Jennifer does have writings she wants to be published, but has not yet to find a publisher.

Much of the poetry that Jennifer writes is done in house on her laptop computer. With the assistance of a program called *Writer*, typing long and thoughtful poems becomes easier to do. By typing one letter Jennifer can choose from a list of words starting with that letter. Typing student letters will allow her to cipher out the words she wants to use.

On May 19th Jennifer's abstract personal interpretation artwork will be on display behind the Drama Department by the Gazebo on the CSU, Stanislaus campus. Along with her artwork her literary poetry will be read along side other works in a ceremony for the 2004 *Penumbra*.

With her spirits high there seems to be nothing Jennifer Kuhn can not accomplish. It's her honest and loving family helping to keep her spirits up as she gets closer to living her dream as a author of children's books. When asked if she would like to work toward obtaining a masters degree Jennifer's humorous response was "I don't need any more letters to go along with my name."

2004 *Penumbra* Reading
Art & Literary Magazine

Date: May 19, 2004
Time: 7:00pm

Free Admission

Even Broken-Winged Divas Can Fly

CSU Stanislaus | News & Events   Page 1 of 2

A-Z Directory | Calendars | Catalog | Class Schedule | Online Learning | Contact Us - Maps |

Quick Links

News & Events

Home > News & Events > News Release

Printer-friendly version

Quadriplegic Alumna Aims to Enlighten Through Writing

Article | September 4, 2012 | By James Leonard

CSU Stanislaus alumna Jennifer Kuhns plans to release her second children's book this fall.

It was the first day of kindergarten — a confusing and nerve-wracking experience for many children, but an entirely new sort of whirlwind for a quadriplegic girl with cerebral palsy.

As Jennifer Kuhns sat outside in her wheelchair, waiting for the start of class — a curious boy turned to her and asked, "Were you born in that chair?"

The simple query became symbolic of the CSU Stanislaus alumna's challenging childhood, and it stuck with her as she grew and progressed through school. And it eventually became the inspiration for — and the title of — her first children's book, which was published in 2010.

"I was bullied," said Kuhns, who went on to earn bachelor's and master's degrees at CSU Stanislaus. "I was treated as deaf, dumb and blind — or just plain stupid. My mom says early on, I developed an odd sense of humor and an acceptance of other peoples' actions toward me."

Born 10 weeks premature in Hollister, Kuhns first began writing while a student at Gavilan Junior College in Gilroy. At CSU Stanislaus, she dove into the study of literature while pursuing a bachelor's degree in English, which she earned while graduating Summa Cum Laude in 2005. Three years later, she completed her master's degree in interdisciplinary studies with an English concentration.

While at CSU Stanislaus, Kuhns was published several times in Penumbra, the campus' annual art and literary journal, and she also worked on the journal's editorial staff. She said that experience was critical in preparing her for life after college, especially the world of publishing.

"It was in the Penumbra class where I learned what I needed to know to deal with editors, publishers, formatting people, and what goes in an advertising package," Kuhns said. "While at CSU Stanislaus, I learned about the benefits of networking and how to network, although networking takes me a bit longer than some."

Kuhns describes herself as "a writer who doesn't physically write." She dictates to her mother, Mitzi, who then types the words on a netbook Jennifer carries everywhere she goes.

In "Were You Born in That Chair?" a girl in a wheelchair helps teach her classmates about disabilities, with one of the key lessons being that all of them had some sort of disability, but most just weren't as visible as hers. The book — which recently won the Mom's Choice Award for family-friendly media, products and services — includes activities and cutouts that Kuhns said have been popular among teachers, and she has visited several local classrooms in addition to other gatherings and book signings to help promote the book and spread its message.

Kuhns hopes to publish her second children's book, "A Box Full of Letters," in the fall, and she's working on a third book that will be more tailored to younger children. She said she hopes the books will teach children to ask questions, be compassionate, and look beyond the surface to get to know people before making judgments.

"I guess what I learned most about growing up as a disabled person is to try everything you can, and don't give up," said Kuhns, who was a 4-H member as a child and showed sheep for nine years. "People can be mean, but that's usually because they don't understand or are afraid. And most of all, laugh."

← GO BACK

http://apps.csustan.edu/news/news_story_full.aspx?WNTNEWS_ID=6395&WNTNEWSD... 7/21/2013

Jennifer Kuhns

Feature

Jennifer Kuhns Leaves No Room For Excuses

"Jenni is a very social person. She always wants to be out and about." – Mitzi Kuhns

Jennifer Kuhns, Award Winning Author, Painter and Poet

Metaphorically stooping down to reach the level of her elementary grade readers, Jennifer Kuhns, award winning author, painter and poet impacts every child—and she does so from her wheelchair.

Her mother, Mitzi Kuhns, transcribes each line of prose by collecting notes as her daughter dictates. They spend hours per week at a local Starbucks, constructing stories for a unique niche.

Kuhns focuses on disabilities, discriminations and prejudices, reaching children of all ages and backgrounds. These fun-loving storylines, permeated with some of life's greatest lessons, have the potential to capture any reader's heart.

Cerebral Palsy, a condition Kuhns has struggled with since birth, has left her a quadriplegic. On top of such severe paralysis, Kuhns also communicates with severe speech impediments.

Her parents, and those closest to her, can usually understand what she's trying to say. For words they get wrong, Kuhns will

22 OAKDALE LIVING MAGAZINE

Even Broken-Winged Divas Can Fly

continue to speak until they are able to comprehend what she's saying.

"I play several different roles in Jenni's life," says her mother, Mitzi. "I am her caregiver, and in this role, she is my boss. We ride that fine line together. There are different roles at different times. We've both learned to go with the flow," she says.

Born three months premature, Kuhns lacked the oxygen her brain needed in order to develop these faculties fully. But in spite of these challenges, she has not let anything stunt her pursuit of artistic dreams.

She proves that no challenge is too great and that every person—regardless of economic status, race, background or disability—every person has something special to contribute.

This perspective is best played out through the stories Kuhns has constructed. In her first book called, "Were You Born in that Chair?" the main character, Hailey, educates her classmates and her teacher on the issue of disabilities.

They realize that we all have imperfections. It encourages the reader to really stop and listen to other people before passing judgment. This particular piece has recently been made available in Spanish as an eBook.

Her second book, a companion to the first called, "A Box Full of Letters," continues with the same protagonist. Hailey and her friends stumble upon a box of old war letters where they come to find out that discrimination is not a new problem but that it's been around for a long time.

In her last published book called, "Hailey's Dream" the disabled protagonist dreams that she is able to get up out of her wheelchair, only to discover that there are several benefits to being in one. Aside

from a refreshing perspective concerning imagination, it gives the reader a unique appreciation for what they have.

In all three stories Kuhns writes with a great amount of depth. History is woven into each narrative. She focuses on inclusion instead of exclusion, often times changing the reader's perspective or imparting something new.

Every piece she writes carries an important take-away. Kuhns has created a muslin pocket doll for "Hailey's Dream" as well as other parent/child activities for each of her other books.

These tools are designed to aid with comprehension and interaction. She's also tackled other writing projects such as re-writing, "A Midsummer Night's Dream," for a fourth-grade level. Other projects are in the works with lessons about bullying and the importance of being you.

On top of these achievements, Kuhns has completed a Master's Degree in Interdisciplinary Studies with an English concentration.

With a great amount of humor and wit, the courage and tenacity of Jennifer Kuhns doesn't leave us with much room for excuses. Her life and work radiate triumph for anybody who desires to touch the life of another person and make a difference. Each of us has our own distinct set of disabilities.

We have a choice to either offer up our own contribution or to sit on the sidelines of life. Kuhns, a valiant young woman, blazes the trail for those of us brave enough to utter even a single word or syllable in the direction of our dreams.

If you'd like more information about Jenni, and how to purchase her books, visit http://www.jenniferkuhns.net.

STORY BY JOANNE REESE   PHOTO BY STEPHEN BROWNING

Once again, front page above-the-fold.

Two members of my Master's Thesis Committee and a couple of my biggest and loudest supporters at CSU Stanislaus

Dr. Armin Schulz (aka Bob), my friend, my mentor, who confirmed that I could do anything

Dr. John Carroll (whom I dubbed "The Robin Williams of the Stanislaus English Department") who never failed to understand my babblistics and never understood why I was the only one who "got" his jokes

Jennifer Kuhns

My very first test-audience for my children's books: my first niece and, nine years later, my one and only co-author to-date

My mother, father, and me with my Michigan family

Jennifer Kuhns

Some of my Tennessee family

and finally, in case you don't believe . . .

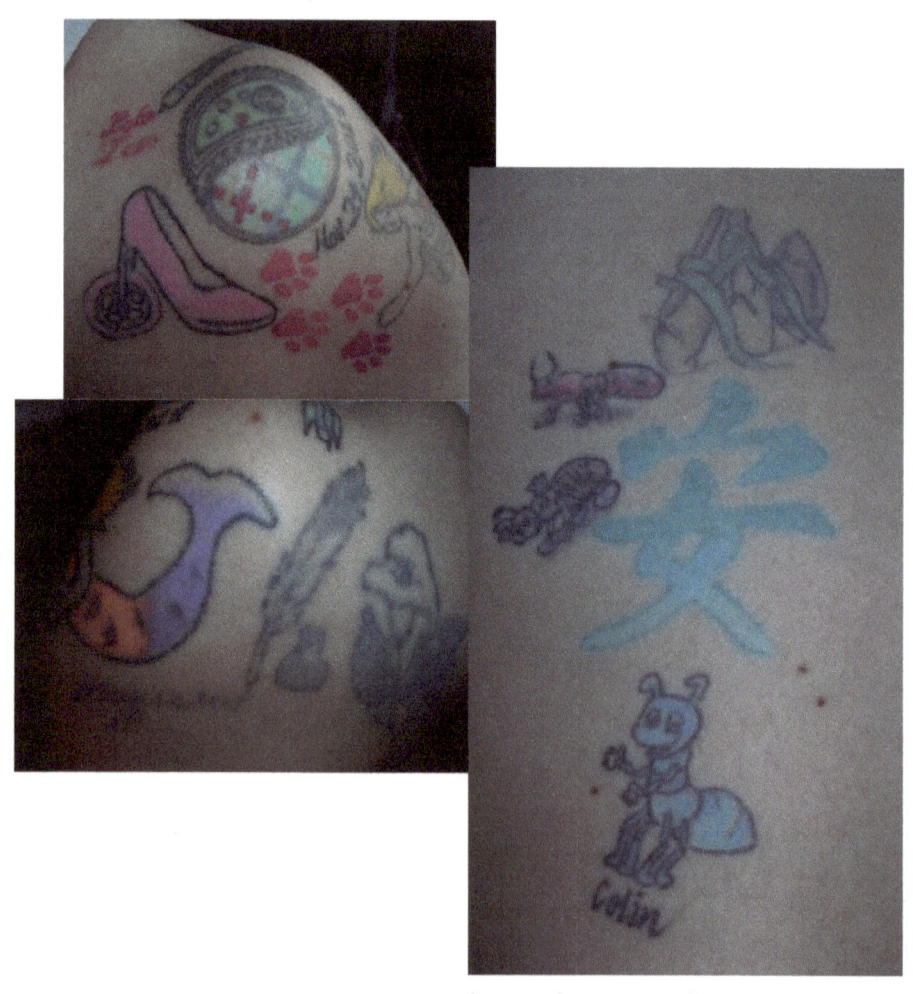

my Body-of-Proof

For other exciting book
by Jennifer Kuhns
Please visit our website at
www.shalakopress.com.

Were You Born In That Chair?

A Box Full Of Letters

Hailey's Dream

Miles To The Moon

Lilly Gets Lucky

Taco

Looking for Lola

Little Diva On Wheels

Paisley or Plaid . . . Being Your Very Best You